INFLUENCE OF CHILDHOOD EXPERIENCES ON FAITH DEVELOPMENT

A JOURNEY TOWARD WHOLENESS

Sr. Adaku Helen Ogbuji, CCVI, Ph.D.

En Route Books and Media, LLC
Saint Louis, MO

ENROUTE
Make the time

En Route Books and Media, LLC
5705 Rhodes Avenue
St. Louis, MO 63109

Contact us at contactus@enroutebooksandmedia.com

Nihil Obstat: Fr. Dr. Austin N. Kanu, J.C.D., Judicial Vicar, Umuahia Diocese, 11th December 2018.

Imprimatur: Most Rev. Dr. Lucius I. Ugorji, D.D., Bishop of Umuahia Diocese, 15th December 2018

ISBN: 979-8-88870-276-5
Library of Congress Control Number:
Available online at https://catalog.loc.gov

First published by Lumen Press, 57 Azikiwe Road, P. O. Box 99, Umuahia, Nigeria, and printed by Franciscan Kolbe Press, P.O. Box 468, 00217 Limuru (Kenya) in 2019.

Dedication

This work is dedicated to
all Religious Men and Women all over the world.

Acknowledgments

This book would not have been completed without God's steady love and indispensable blessings. I thank God for guiding me at every step.

I am grateful to my Congregation Leadership Team and all the Sisters of Charity of the Incarnate Word of Houston, Texas, for their prayers and support.

My former bishop, Most Rev. Dr. Lucius I. Ugorji, granted the *Imprimatur* to this work. I appreciate his support and kind heart. I also thank Very Rev. Dr. Austin N. Kanu for reviewing the work and granting the *Nihil Obstat* for its publication.

My mother, Fidelia Lucy Ogbuji, and my siblings, Fr. Udo, Gloria, Henry, and Prisca, are wonderful to me. I thank them for their warm love and inspiration. I cherish the gentle love of my late father, Joseph Ogbuji, who gave me love and taught me how to care for others in love. The love of my nephews, Chigozie, Akachukwu, Enyioma, Chimdike, Gerald, Greg, and my niece, Amarachi, has added a special flavor to my life, and I'm grateful to them.

My relatives and friends walked with me on this journey, and I thank them from my heart. I thank my cousin Joy, my sister-in-law Nkiru, Uncle Austin Igbuku, Sir Pius Ogiji, Fr. Dr. Reginald Temu, and Fr. Brian Treacy. I thank Fr. Dr. Emmanuel Foro, SJ, for writing the preface and Dr. Steve Asatsa for writing the foreword. I am grateful to Lumen Press for publishing this work for the first time and Franciscan Kolbe Press for designing and printing it in 2019. I appreciate En Route Books and Media, especially Dr. Sebastian Mahfood, OP, for republishing it in 2024. You are all dear to me; thank you!

Finally, I am indebted to all the individuals who generously shared their stories and participated in the extensive research that made this book possible. I am especially thankful to the eighty religious men and women who were interviewed during this process. As the list of those who contributed to this work is extensive, I carry your names not in ink, but forever in my grateful heart. I pray God to reward you with his peace and favor.

Table of Contents

Foreword

Influence of Childhood Experiences on Faith Development: A Journey Toward Wholeness is a timely piece of work. It gives a holistic approach to the process of religious formation and consecration. It conceptualizes the consecration process from a threefold approach. The book uncovers the process of formation as a mentor-mentee relationship where a formee receives spiritual guidance and accompaniment from the formator as he/she discerns God's will. This process culminates in a lifestyle where the formed person hears from God with clarity and does His will.

The book explores early childhood experiences and faith development in the formative years of consecrated persons. This is highly innovative as it brings out the foundation of the humanness of religious persons on which adulthood character is built. With this being a neglected aspect in religious formation, the author demonstrates the importance of the past in understanding the present and future.

The book revolutionizes the process of consecration by integrating the formators' spiritual work plan with the formees' individual past experiences. It integrates spirituality and humanness as inseparable and vital domains in the process of becoming consecrated. The book attempts to interpret the relationship between the past experiences and adult behavior of religious men and women and clearly demonstrates their interdependence in shaping consecrated life. This conceptualization of the religious person as a whole rather than the sum of disintegrated domains brings new knowledge in the self-awareness and understanding of religious men and women. This will play a vital role in enhancing the service of religious persons to God and humanity.

Finally, acknowledging the relationship between childhood experiences and faith development among consecrated persons, the book suggests therapeutic approaches that could enhance the formation process. The author recognizes the human as not only a spiritual being but also a biopsychospiritual being. The psychological approaches would enrich the process of formation, which has been conceptualized in this book as a lifelong process.

I highly recommend this book to religious men and women, superiors and formators, clergy and lay persons, and all those who wish to understand how their childhood experiences affect their behavior as adults. This book is an idea whose time has come!

Dr. Stephen Asatsa,
Head of Department, (HOD)
Department of Counselling Psychology,
The Catholic University of Eastern Africa, Kenya

Preface

Formation to Consecrated Life has been defined in this book according to the two meanings of *initial* and *ongoing*. Within both of these levels, childhood experiences hold an influential place, just as the foundation of a building holds an important role in the safe use of the whole edifice. While for centuries, most Catholics believed more in the power of grace coming from the call to follow Jesus through the practice of the evangelical counsels, the progress in the human sciences led us slowly to realize the common root of human needs and ambitions in life.

The Second Vatican Council gave a strong hint in the fifth chapter of *Lumen Gentium* by presenting the universal call to holiness addressed to all constituencies of the one Church, each according to the measure of grace received and the call heard and accepted. From the Anthropology of Christian Vocation to newer publications in the field of human development, the human person now occupies the central stage and plays a greater role. This is not expressing a kind of 'death of God' but a more sober understanding of the perfecting role of grace over nature, as the human person is taking full stock of what his or her contribution consists of in the great divine work of salvation and sanctification.

In the various definitions of faith that define this book, one could include a nuanced version indicating that faith is in part a deep 'self-acceptance' and the absolute acceptance of God the Creator, Redeemer, and Sanctifier. God reveals Himself to us to help us know God, the world, and ourselves, among other creatures of God. God reveals Himself through Nature, Culture, Scripture, and Spirit. Sister

Helen draws on this progress to contribute to the formation work of religious and consecrated persons as they consider the real characteristics of this nature on which grace works for its perfection in Christ.

This human nature is never isolated from its social location or historical development. We are our biological makeup, just as we are our personal history of relations. The primary significant others in a human life are the parents or initial caretakers. To them is entrusted the treasures of our future. This 'faith of God' in human freedom stands as a total mystery that no Theology will ever explain to the satisfaction of all, but it is a symbol of God's respect for the human person who is not only bent on wrong-doing, but primarily capable of prodigy in the world. The mystery of our interdependence for individual fulfilment is revisited when the role of these first caregivers in personal life is highlighted in its positive and negative impact on the journey toward holiness. In the current context, we are talking about consecrated life, but this early-stage relationship operates in similar ways for all vocations in life. Being able to answer these questions: What am I historically made of? Who are the people who made my childhood? These questions amount to coming closer to the truth of my actual being.

For the formation to consecrated life, in consecrated life, and through consecrated life, it makes a world of difference: to know that I can attain holiness by presenting myself before the Lord just as I am, that is with my brokenness and with my strengths. My glory and my misery, on the scene of my actual history, play their respective roles in my thought and action patterns—in all regards. With these indeed, grace engages a stupendous fight in the process of formation. It is, therefore, necessary for formators to be more aware of these realities of the human soul in view of better accompanying the unending process of sanctification through the life of the evangelical counsels in their formees, and for leaders to facilitate the ongoing dimension of this same formation. Therapy, loving awareness, deeper self-acceptance through self-knowledge, growth in social and relational skills, and learning appropriate responses to life challenges could be a few names of this spiritual development for religious and consecrated persons.

God does not always provide miraculous healing in a literal sense, but the joy of embracing humanity as expressed through one's unique experience opens the possibility of forming communities of sharing in life and of joy. Embracing my humanity means embracing humanity in short, and we remember that the "glory of God is human fully alive" and fully human before God.

This book is a must-read for formators of religious congregations and Institutes of Consecrated and Apostolic Life. Superiors of the same communities will also find it insightful and positive about the universal need for therapy defined as greater self-acceptance and self-management with the help of others under God's guidance. Pastors of souls can greatly benefit from this condensed text on reconciling with one's own joy and suffering, finding healing through a trained "wounded healer," in line with God's Incarnation. All consecrated persons will find delight in discovering the wide range of possibilities in the helping professions. Finally, believers with a strong scientific background will rejoice in the continuous line between faith and the human sciences around the soul, which is a joint of body and spirit in a person.

In short, this book will help any reader to feel more comfortable with the concept of psychological health. The very fine line argues in favour of this vital link between the body and the spirit. Physical and spiritual well-being depends significantly on psychological well-being in just the same way as the latter strives on the former. We are, however, warned against secularity and scientific idolatry, for neither the process nor the helper alone heals. It is rather the spirit in persons entering the helping relationship that provides the opportunity for healing to take place. Simply said, God heals through human mediation and faithfulness, and through a trusting spirit.

Fr. Dr. Emmanuel Foro, SJ,
Rector, Hekima University College,
Nairobi, Kenya

Definition of Key Terms

Religious or a Consecrated Person: In this book, the term Religious person/s is used interchangeably with Consecrated person/s. This work follows the definition of the Code of Canon Law on who a religious person is. According to Canon Law, a religious person is a man or woman who is consecrated by the profession of the evangelical counsels of poverty, chastity, and obedience and who follows Christ more closely under the action of the Holy Spirit, and is totally dedicated to God who is loved most of all, for the upbuilding of the Church and the salvation of the world (can. 573, #1).

Religious or Consecrated Life: In this work, consecrated or religious life is the life embraced by the love of God, and it manifests in the Church as a wonderful marriage brought about by God (can. 573, #1). It is a way of life that requires individuals to dedicate themselves to God for their entire existence. This lifestyle is typically followed within religious congregations, institutes of consecrated life, and societies of apostolic life. Such sacrifice requires them to continue worshipping God with love in their radical and prophetic vowed way of life. Religious life is open to all Catholics who are prepared to embrace the way of life of the religious order or institute they wish to join. The Canon law states that religious life is for any Catholic, endowed with a right intention who has the qualities required by universal and proper law and who is not prevented by any impediment (can. 597, #1). These impediments are:

1. One who has not yet completed seventeen years of age,
2. A spouse, while the marriage continues to exist,
3. One who is currently bound by a sacred bond to some institute of consecrated life or is incorporated in some society of apostolic life,
4. One who enters the institute induced by force, grave fear, or malice, or the one whom a superior, induced in the same way,
5. One who has concealed his or her incorporation in some institute of consecrated life or in some society of apostolic life (can 643, #1).

The vocation to consecrated life in the Catholic Church is a call to sacrificial love, self-surrender, and self-emptying.

Religious formation: This work defines religious formation as a process by which an intended candidate is guided by a formator, to discern God's will in their expectation to serve Him. The candidate known as the "formee" is helped by the formator to progress in spiritual matters and how to actually live a religious life in God's service. Religious formation leads a formee to actively discern God's will and accordingly respond to his call. Discernment and a prayerful life play a vital role in the formation of a candidate. This includes understanding and approaching the will of God, as well as nurturing an early desire to serve into a strong passion for God's love and ministry.

There are two main stages of religious formation: Initial formation and On-going formation. The initial formation consists of the initial stages of learning the constitution, the way of life of a congregation, the meaning of religious life, the Scripture, Catholic Social Teachings, community living, the vows, etc. Initial formation starts from Postulancy to temporary professed religious life, which some congregations call juniors, scholastics, or religious in annual vows. The ongoing formation is for religious in perpetual vows and is no longer under formal formation. It is believed that formation lasts throughout life, and thus, each professed religious person continues to learn and grow throughout life (Can. 661).

Community: Each religious person lives with other religious members in a house designated for their common life, known as a religious community. The community is guided by its constitution, spirituality, and the charism of its founder and founding members. In the community, religious members live out their vowed commitment and share things in common.

Faith in this work is not only about the divine gift of trust and confidence in God; it encompasses the value and trust a child develops in self and in the significant other at a tender age. This helps them find meaning in life, develop self-confidence, and build trust in others.

Childhood: When does childhood end? This is a hard question to answer. Childhood is the age span ranging from birth to adolescence (Corsaro, 2005, 191). For the purpose of this book, childhood spans from infancy to adolescence, i.e., from 0 to 18 years of age.

Childhood Experiences: These experiences can be positive or negative. They consist of consistent care, love, and/or stressful or traumatic events, including abuse and neglect, which influence a child's life and may consequently shape their adult life.

CHAPTER ONE

Introduction

"While pain is probably inevitable in life, those who are joyful, despite the pain, are persons whose expectations are right, those who are able to let go and forgive, and those who remain positive."

—Sr. Helena Ogbuji, CCVI

The journey toward wholeness and healing is challenging. It is lonely, painful, depressing, and fearful. We often fear embarking on this journey because we are afraid to confront the unpleasantness of our past and reopen wounds we thought were already healed. At times, we may not even realize that we need healing, and we may be unaware of how our past painful experiences unconsciously affect our behavior as adults.

My father passed away when I was a young girl, which filled me with constant anger toward God, my father, and anyone who spoke about their own father. I missed his love and was very angry with him for dying. I developed a phobia of death, and I feared viewing a dead body. I never knew that I had not buried him, even as an adult. I was still hoping he would return one day. Thus, whenever people talked about their father, I would get angry and go to my room to cry. I remember when I was a teenager, my friend was narrating how her father would buy meat on weekends for her family. I was so upset that day, and I ended up crying bitterly for the entire weekend.

I had never wanted to share this experience with my therapist until one day, she asked me to tell her about my father and how he died. I cried very much during the session and could not narrate the story. She accompanied me until the day I decided to lay him to rest and bury him. It was a very painful and daunting ritual. However, my therapist guided me through the process, and with the grace of God, I embarked on that dreadful journey.

That night, I had a beautiful dream of my father visiting me. He was wearing a beautiful but contagious smile that I still remember with nostalgia. I was so happy to see him. He hugged me and told me that he loved me. That was a grace-filled way to reconcile my childhood experience of phobia of death and my anger toward my father. I woke up very exhausted and worn out but very joyful and fulfilled. I felt different within, and I was never the same again, especially with my incessant anger toward him. After that experience, I loved my father even more, and I enjoyed talking about him to anyone who cared to listen to my story. From my healing experience and through the grace of God, I learned how to die. According to Morrie in *Tuesdays With Morrie*, "When you learn how to die, you learn how to live" (Albom, 2007, P. 104).

Another experience of a journey toward wholeness was embarked on by a priest whom I shall call Fr. James. Fr. James was born into a family of many siblings. Before his conception, there were already four siblings following each other every year. When the mother became pregnant with him, she felt sad and angry about expecting another baby so soon. The child picked up this anger and sadness from the mother's womb. Some people may doubt how this is possible. However, science has demonstrated that by 8 weeks after fertilization, an unborn child can react to touch, and at least 20 weeks, an unborn child can feel pain and recoil from painful experiences (US Congressional Record, 2012, Vol. 158, p. 12852; Gupta, Kilby, & Cooper, 2008, p. 74).

As an adult, the experience of anger and rejection was reflected in the way Fr. James related to God and his immediate family members. He confessed:

> I feel rejected, especially by those closest to me. I react irrationally or angrily in my heart, even though my head tells me that there is no reason for this reaction. I have been experiencing tension and confusion, which leaves me with emotions that I don't understand and struggle to handle. This is often followed by feelings of guilt about these negative moods. I've always had these strange feelings towards my parents, brothers, and sisters, even when I was a priest. I knew they were nonsense, but there was nothing I could do about them. If I left the house, the mood would leave me, and then return as soon as I came back. Subsequently, my image of God was much more cruel and sadistic than that of ordinary earthly fathers. If I felt rejected by my parents, brothers, and sisters (and for me, this was very real but only in my subconscious), then the probability is that I project this same rejection onto God, who is also a father/mother/brother/sister relationship with me.

Fr. James knew he needed an inner healing and this came about through God's grace in dreams and through therapy. He explained:

> In my dream, I was at home as a kid, cutting a hedge with big clippers. I bit into a really big branch, and cut right through it. Suddenly, I found that it was not a branch that I had cut, but I had decapitated a man. I jumped back in horror; his head fell to the ground, and his body began to twitch around on the ground. I screamed. I was horrified. My parents, brothers, and sisters came running out of the house, and they all started laughing and jeering at me.

His therapist guided him through this dream with these interpretations: "Everything in the dream is you in some symbolic way. So, your head is separated from your heart and from your emotions. Could the rejection you felt manifest in the jeering of your family members?"

Reflecting on these interpretations, Fr. James asked himself: "Is it that in some way perhaps my head and my body had been separated from each other? Is it possible that I had stifled my emotions? Could it be from some hurtful experiences or incidents from childhood? Had I ever been hurt, put down, or rejected as a child? Yeah! That is exactly how I have always felt about myself in some way," he expressed. This awareness was the beginning of his journey toward wholeness.

Fr. James went back to his childhood and asked questions. He discovered that his pregnancy was somehow rejected by the mother. His therapist guided him to the womb of his mother. He explained:

> I tried to imagine myself in the womb, and immediately, the scary image of me in the hell comes to my mind. I felt very

> much alone and cut off. The nightmare I had was very vivid. The voice I heard sounded like the voice of my mother crying. I felt totally abandoned and rejected. It was dark. She seemed to be saying – 'I don't want you. I can't cope with yet another child. I've been through more than I can take. These children are taking too much out of me. I'm drained, times are hard.' I tried to imagine the scene of my birth; I knew my parents were sad at my arrival. I just knew that I was not wanted, and I couldn't even bear the sight of myself when I was born. I was so ugly.

Fr. James went through a terrifying journey toward wholeness guided by his therapist and the grace of Christ. Today, he is progressing in psychological healing from this rejection, anger, insecurity, and the feeling of being unloved and unwanted. Fr. James never ceases to praise God through Jesus, the greatest Healer who accompanied him on the journey toward healing and wholeness.

Evidently, the stories above illustrate how one can experience healing grace from God by embarking on a journey toward wholeness after becoming aware of the impact of unhappy childhood experiences.

The experience of counseling many religious persons these many years has exposed me to the challenges that religious persons go through due to the influence of childhood experiences. While many find life meaningful and are happy, responsible, and can easily adapt to a new environment, others seem to manifest a feeling of bitterness or depression, with incessant anger and frequent mood swings. Some of them regress and unconsciously resort to attention-seeking behaviors and cannot take responsibility as adults.

While some religious persons develop unhealthy attachments toward their community members or their formator, others manifest aggressive attitudes toward their community members, and others bully the vulnerable members among them in the form of verbal attacks like gossip, intimidation, name-calling, destructive criticism, or the use of foul language. Some people form closed groups to give the impression that their tribe is superior (ethnocentrism), while others use passive-aggressive behavior to communicate their anger. These attitudes are consciously or unconsciously exhibited to create a sense of security that leads to fear, harm, or distress by a member or group of members directed toward less powerful member(s) in the community.

Some formators also exhibit some of the above behavior toward the formees as well as toward their community members. Sometimes, the formees play the role of the formator when the formator's developmental stages are highly influenced by adverse childhood experiences. This situation could lead to feelings of insecurity, depression, low self-image, and incessant fear. Sometimes, the formees who exhibit these maladjustment behaviors are dismissed from religious life because the formator does not understand the root cause of the problem or how to help them. Other times, the formees make the decision to leave religious life because they are not at home with themselves and others and are not empowered to deal with their issues.

Below are a few examples of how the environment can nurture the way we behave in religious communities.

Once in the community, a consecrated person was constantly packing her few clothes and always ready to leave religious life. At home, she watched her mother frequently pack up and leave home whenever she was physically abused by her father. As a result, she learned unconsciously that she had to be ready at all times in case she experienced conflict with her community leader.

A religious person who was raised by his single mother developed an insecure attachment. Upon joining religious life, he displayed the same insecure attachment to the "mother figure" in their community. He yearned for the same level of care and attention from the community leader as he received from his mother.

Another religious person grew up witnessing physical abuse by his father toward his mother. As a result, he developed incessant anger and became somewhat violent. He developed a mistrust for authority figures.

Another religious person was raised by her stepmother, who disliked her and was cruel to her. She was mistreated and sometimes starved. When she cried, she was forbidden to do so and was even punished for it. This emotional deprivation led to behaviors like fainting and seeking attention through passive means. Her sisters assumed that she was introverted. She was easily agitated and preferred to sit in a corner, whether in their community or outside of the community. She discovered later that her experience with her stepmother impacted her. In their home, she always sat at the corner, especially when her stepmother was around.

A consecrated person grew up in a poor family with his siblings and mother. The family had to share one plate of food, and there wasn't always enough to go around. The older siblings would eat quickly, leaving little for the consecrated person. To ensure he had enough to eat, the mother began saving a portion of food for him, which she would give to him after the older siblings had left the house. This behavior became a daily routine when he was younger. Thus, when the eating time was over, he knew there was a hidden food waiting for him to enjoy. The intention of the mother was to save him from malnutrition and hunger, but this adult religious person grew up knowing that hiding food is normal. In their religious community, whenever it was his turn to cook, he would hide a plate of food for himself and eat later in his room. Even when he was not the cook, he would always save some leftover food in his room. Unconsciously, the community became his home, where food might not always be enough, and he had to hide food to be eaten later.

The list of wounded individuals caused by childhood experiences can go on and on. Sometimes, the consecrated persons appear to society as pure, perfect, and free from stress. No wonder some of the laity frequently request the religious to pray for them, while oblivious of the fact that those who live consecrated life need prayers too. Some religious, who are unconsciously and unintentionally driven by childhood traumatic experiences, may not be aware of how much these experiences are shielded under their religious garbs/habits. These hidden motivators and secret prompts may cause some to abscond from religious life or to live an unhappy life as consecrated individuals. Certainly, the scars from the past remind us of where we have been. But, are they to dictate where we are going? Our past stories should only inform us, but not define us!

In their statistics, the Secretary of Congregation for Institutes of Consecrated Life and Societies of Apostolic Life, Archbishop José

Rodríguez Carballo, explained in his address on the 29th of October 2013 that statistics from his Congregation, the Congregation for the Doctrine of the Faith, as well as the Congregation for the Clergy, indicated that in the past five years, more than 3,000 religious per year have chosen to leave the consecrated life (Carballo, 2013). On January 28, 2017, Pope Francis called this desertion from religious life and lack of vocation to religious life, a "haemorrhage of vocations to the consecrated life" or "abandonment of vocations" during his address to members of the Congregation for the Institutes of Consecrated Life and the Societies of Apostolic Life (Catholic World News, January 28, 2017).

The document released in 2017 by the Congregation for Institutes of Consecrated Life and Societies of Apostolic Life, entitled: *New Wine in New Wineskins: The Consecrated Life and Its Ongoing Challenges since Vatican II*, noted with dismay the persistent high number of those leaving the consecrated life (no. 12). The document explained that the reason for this crisis of faith is as a result of "the deviation between what is proposed in terms of values and what is actually lived and the disappointment experienced in living an inauthentic common life."

It has been illustrated that most of these cases occur at a "relatively young age." The causes include an "absence of spiritual life," "loss of a sense of community," and a "loss of sense of belonging to the Church" and affective problems (Carballo, 2013). Pope Francis attributed the abandonment of vocations to materialism, moral relativism, easy money and pleasure desired by the youth, and the counter testimony found in consecrated life (Catholic World News,

2017). Consequently, the departure from consecrated life is observable in every cultural and geographical context and among not only those in the initial stages of formation but also among those in perpetual vows (Carballo and Braz de Aviz, 2017, no. 12).

As religious people, we are called to find grace in living religious life and to support and lift each other up patiently. At times, our wounds get in the way. Gitau (2016) expressed:

> Some religious come from dysfunctional families and deformed cultural norms and may live unstable forms of life in the Institutes; some do not know how to relate with people, how to deal with conflict, or cope with stress; some lack in-depth prayer life; while some take to witchcraft when faced with insecurity or existential issues. (p. 144)

This is not surprising since these individuals are formed by the wealth of experiences and attitudes of their families. Reporting for Kenya *Daily Nation* on March 27th, Okeyo (2017) enlightened that 13.1% of children aged 0-14 live without parental care, 38% of orphans end up in charity homes, and 250,000 children live and work on the street. Okeyo enumerated the number of cases of abuse of children that were reported between January and December 2016: Neglected cases of children-313 cases, Abandonment-78 cases, sexual abuse-303 cases, physical abuse-356 cases, emotional abuse-44 cases, abduction-23 cases, early marriage-82 cases, trafficking-16 cases, child labour-18 cases, and prostitution-2 cases. In 2016, 1296 cases of child abuse were reported. In Nairobi alone, 255 cases of child abuse and neglect were reported between January and March of 2017.

These cases largely reflect the societal context from which potential future candidates for consecrated life may emerge. With the background of such experiences of their wounded nature and life experiences, are there avenues set up among religious congregations for healing these wounds? Religious individuals should be aware that families are the first school of any individual. These young individuals come with a range of experiences and pre-existing attitudes shaped by their family backgrounds, some of which require adjustment and transformation.

Certainly, many candidates who wish to join consecrated life come from dysfunctional and broken homes. Some of them have experienced traumatic events such as divorce, parental separation, war, political violence, abuse (physical, sexual, or emotional), rape, natural disasters, tribal conflicts, parental neglect, child labor, etc. Thus, there is a need to integrate the formees' broken past history into their beautiful call to religious life through an integrated formation process (Maganya, 2016, p. 145).

The Beauty of the Life and Insatiable Attitude in Religious Life

Religious life manifests in the Church as a wonderful marriage brought about by God, a sign of the future age, and religious people bring to perfection their full gift as a sacrifice to God. (can. 573, #1). Schneiders (2013) compares religious life with the parable of the Hidden Treasure and the Pearl narrated by Jesus in Matthew 13:44.

According to her, religious life is a treasure that a person found hidden in a field, out of joy, sold all she had in order to buy that field (p. 1).

The beauty of religious life is that it ought to be a life of joy—the joy of bringing God's consolation to all people. Religious people are called to be bearers of this message of joy and hope, says Pope Francis (*Rejoice*, no. 3). The Pope continues: "Religious are to give serenity and joy, God's consolation, and his tenderness to all. But if religious persons first experience the joy of being consoled by God, of being loved by Him, then they can bring that joy to others." Indeed, happiness in one's life depends on the quality of one's thoughts, on contentment, and self-acceptance.

This reminds me of a story:

> A king, who, despite his luxurious lifestyle, was neither happy nor contented. One day the king came upon a servant who was singing happily while he worked. This fascinated the king as to why he, the supreme ruler of the land, was unhappy and gloomy while a lowly servant was so happy. The king asked the servant: "Why are you so happy?" The man replied: "Your majesty, I am nothing but a servant, but my family and I don't need too much - just a roof over our heads and warm food to fill our tummies." The king was not satisfied with that reply.
>
> Later on that day, he sought the advice of his most trusted advisor. After hearing the king's woes and the servant's story, the advisor said: "Your majesty, I believe that the servant has not been made a part of the 99 Club." "The 99

Club? And what exactly is that?" the king enquired. The advisor replied: "Your majesty, to truly know what the 99 Club is all about, place 99 gold coins in a bag and leave it at the servant's doorsteps." When the servant saw the bag, he took it into his house. When he opened the bag, he let out a great shout of joy...so many gold coins! He began to count them. After several counts, he was at last convinced that there were 99 coins. He wondered, "What could have happened to that last gold coin? Surely, no one would leave 99 coins!" He looked everywhere he could, but the final coin was elusive. Finally exhausted, he decided that he was going to work harder than ever to earn that gold coin and complete his collection.

From that day, the servant's life changed. He was overworked, horribly gloomy, and castigated his family for not helping him make that 100th gold coin. He stopped singing while he worked. Witnessing this dramatic transformation, the king was puzzled. When he sought his advisor's advice and help, the advisor said: "Your majesty, the servant has now officially joined the 99 Club." He continues, "The 99 Club is a name given to those who have enough to be happy but are never contented because they are always yearning and striving for that extra one gold, telling themselves: "Let me get that one final thing, then I will be happy for life" (Paul, M. K., *Achieving Personal Greatness*).

Some consecrated individuals have strayed from their chosen life of poverty and have joined this 99th club to pursue financial security and investments, losing touch with their charism and spirituality. And my question is: Whom are we investing for? This lack of commitment to our charism and mission is resulting in greed, jealousy, competition, materialism, and avarice within religious communities. It is clear that human desires and needs are limitless and insatiable. Certainly, we can find happiness and contentment with very little in our lives. However, when we start seeking something bigger and better, our desires grow, causing us to lose sleep and happiness. Sometimes, this pursuit can lead us to hurt the people around us. It can even breed enmity, starting from a small spark of jealousy or envy and growing to the point where it consumes our lives. This hostility sometimes destroys religious communities. Actually, there is no holiness in sadness, in bitterness, in resentment, in hostility, or in gloomy disposition. "Bitterness is not Christian. Pain is, but not bitterness," says Pope Francis. Sadness and greed must, therefore, give way to joy and contentment.

Religious people are called to radiate joy in their respective orders, congregations, or institutes, in their ministries, and in the whole world rather than living bitter and unsatisfied lives. No wonder Pope Francis asked religious persons to wake up the world. During his meeting with the Union of Superiors General on November 29th, 2013, Pope Francis resounded: "Religious life promotes growth in the church by way of attraction. The Church must be attractive. Wake up the world! Be witnesses of a different way of doing things, of acting, of living! It is this witness that I expect of you. Religious should be men and women who are able to wake the world up."

Unfortunately, some consecrated individuals are bitter, depressed, highly aggressive, and reliant on alcohol, which serves as a temporary balm to alleviate their wounds, pain and loneliness. Unforgiveness and heavy grudges are also eating many up like cancer. Religious people cannot radiate joy or wake up the world when they have not taken care of the baggage of hatred, petty jealousy, resentment, gossip, unforgiveness, greed, tribal sentiment, etc., that are hanging on their shoulders. Actually, the heaviest thing a religious can carry is a grudge. When these wounds are healed, religious persons can authentically witness radically to the life of joy, love, beauty, and hope they are called to.

The Experience of Formation in Religious Life:

Apart from the Catholic basic teachings and the congregation's values, way of life, and spirituality; the formation process to religious life is intended also to take care of personal trauma sustained through prenatal or postnatal adverse experiences, as well as the inherited parental wounds, addictions, rejections, abuses, and all kinds of childhood adverse experiences. Unfortunately, one gets the impression that the formation process is more informative (Carballo and Braz de Aviz, 2017, no.12) rather than transformative.

A candidate who aspires to a religious life and carries the wound of rejection from parents will join a consecrated life that seems to promise a joyful and good life. This formee may, unfortunately, encounter other wounded religious, and the religious community will become a home for sick and bitter people. On the other hand, if the journey to wholeness began during the initial stages of formation, healing can start taking place through the grace of God.

The question to ask is: Is our formation process transforming candidates or deforming them? Are formators holistically trained? Do formators know the prenatal and postnatal stories that may have influenced candidates' behavior? And if they do know, do they have the skills to help these candidates? Are there options for counseling and spiritual direction?

Carballo (2017) noted:

> Many institutes lack members who are adequately trained and prepared for the ministry of formation. Without a solid formation of formators, it would not be possible to provide a true and promising accompaniment to the young people who seek to join religious life. Congregations should take great care when choosing consecrated men and women as formators. (no. 16)

The scenario below supports Carballo's fear:

Once, in a formation house, a new candidate was invited to say grace before a meal. She began with a "Hail Mary." The formator shouted at her and told her not to mention the name of that "woman" again. The new candidate was flabbergasted, shocked, and wondered how a formator could be afraid to hear the name of Mary, the Mother of Jesus. Because formation is the bedrock of every religious institute's life, religious congregations and societies of apostolic life must seriously examine their formation programs and processes and carefully select formation personnel.

Religious formation is basically for any Catholic who wishes to join consecrated life. This involves a program on spirituality, theology, scripture, psychology, human development, Catholic Social Teachings, etc. Sometimes formees go through the formation process without experiencing transformation. However, the primary goal of religious formation, according to the Congregation for Institutes of Consecrated Life and Societies of Apostolic Life, is to permit candidates to religious life and young professed religious, first, to discover and, later, to assimilate and deepen that which religious identity consists. Only under these conditions will the person dedicated to God be inserted into the world as a significant, effective, and faithful witness.

Indeed, no one can be admitted to religious life without adequate preparation. Through the grace of the Holy Spirit and the formation process, each religious person progresses in their spiritual or religious life and in discerning God's will for them. To know what God wants is a first step, and it is indeed the first objective in formation. The next step, and one which is taken in conjunction with discerning God's will, is to do what God wants.

This period is characterized by ceaseless prayer, thorough preparation, and formation that lasts from three to four years, depending on the institute, before the person makes the first or temporary profession of vows. The preparations or the formation stages are left in the hands of each Congregation (Can.597). The common stages include:

- Postulancy (pre-novitiate) (Renovationis Causa 1917, nos. 539-541)
- Novitiate
- Temporal vows
- Perpetual vows

The right to admit any individual into any stage of formation, from the postulancy stage to the perpetual profession, is vested in the leaders of the congregation according to their constitution. Can. 645 explains that with vigilant care, superiors are only to admit those who, besides the required age, have the health, suitable character, and sufficient qualities of maturity to embrace the proper life of the institute. Indeed, health, character, and maturity are to be verified even by using experts. They must show proof of baptism, confirmation, and free status from marriage.

There are two main stages of religious formation: Initial formation and ongoing formation. As the name implies, the initial formation consists of the initial stages of learning the constitution, the way of life of the congregation, prayer, spirituality, and charism, the meaning of religious life, community living, the vows, as well as learning deeply the Catholic faith, the moral teachings of the Church, reading and praying with the Scriptures, the liturgy of the hours, Eucharist, etc. On the other hand, ongoing formation begins after a religious person has made the perpetual profession. Since formation is a lifelong process, the individual continues to update themselves with available resources and training for continued growth.

During the initial formation process, each formee moves from one stage of formation to another as they prayerfully discern where God wants them to serve. With proper discernment, a postulant becomes a novice. Actually, it is during the novitiate stage that religious life begins, and this stage is not to last longer than two years, and, with permission, six months can be added when necessary (O'Reilly, 2013, p.125; compare Can. 648, §3). After these two years are over, a novice is allowed to make first vows when:

1. The person who is to make it has completed at least eighteen years of age;
2. The novitiate has been validly completed;
3. Admission has been given freely by the competent superior with the vote of the council according to the norm of law;
4. The profession is expressed and made without force, grave fear, or malice;
5. The profession is received by a legitimate superior personally or through another (Can. 656).

When the novice makes first vows, the family members, friends, well-wishers, extended family members, and other members of the congregation celebrate this joyful occasion. The consecrated persons in annual vows live in religious communities where they continue to be formed and serve within the congregation. In every religious institute, the formation of the members is to be continued after the first profession so that they can fully embrace the values of the institute and effectively carry out its mission. During this initial formation, the temporary professed person is under a formator until she makes perpetual vows.

The Role of Ongoing Formation

A religious in temporary vows will request to make perpetual vows according to the constitution of the said congregation after attaining 21 years of age and having lived as a temporary professed member for at least three years and not more than nine years (Can. 657-658). Religious who have made perpetual or solemn vows are regarded as religious on an ongoing formation and are no longer under formal formation. However, each institute is obligated to organize courses on theology, spirituality, human development, community living, and values of the said order to continue to educate its professed members. Carballo (2017) explains that it is urgent that a culture of ongoing formation be put in place for all religious institutes, which include not only the elucidation of theoretical concepts, but also the evaluation and verification of a community's lived experience (no.16).

Formation is believed to last throughout life because it is a process of growing into Christian maturity (Ezeani, 2017). Being a *process* implies that it is gradual and lasts throughout life.

> A story is told of John, a woodcutter, who worked for a company for 5 years but never got a raise. The company hired Bill, and within a year, he got a raise. Then John resented Bill's getting a raise after just one year and went to his boss

> to talk about it. The boss said, "You are still cutting the same number of trees you were cutting 5 years ago. We are a result-oriented company and would be happy to give you a raise if your productivity goes up." John went back and started hitting harder and putting in longer hours, but he still wasn't able to cut more trees. He went back to his boss and told him of his dilemma. The boss told him to go talk to Bill, "Maybe there is something that Bill knows that you and I don't." John went and asked Bill how he managed to cut more trees. Bill answered, "After every tree I cut, I take a break for 2 minutes and sharpen my axe. When was the last time you sharpened your axe?" "Oh, five years ago," said John. (Khera, 2014)

As religious, we have to continuously sharpen the axe of our lives through an ongoing formation process. When was the last time you attended a seminar or workshop for continuing education as a consecrated person? Religious persons can become stagnant when they stop learning. Just as we feed our stomachs every day with food for physical energy, our minds also need to be sharpened with ongoing training. Thus, each perpetually professed religious person could continue to learn and grow throughout life.

Collins (2017) explains that the "discernment process does not end when one enters the convent but continues as one progresses through the various stages of formation. Unlike marriage, which by its nature must be permanent and exclusive from the very start, religious life does not acquire permanency until solemn vows have been professed." Can. 661 further echoes, "Through their entire life, religious are to continue diligently their spiritual, doctrinal, and practical formation. Superiors, moreover, are to provide them with the resources and time for this." This continuous formation helps a religious person to develop a deeper faith, as well as become spiritually and emotionally grounded to live a religious life fully and in union with the Person of Jesus Christ.

Blanhette and Maloney (2009) explain that for formation discernment to be authentic, five processes are imperative and guide the process: being attentive to the movement of the Holy Spirit within an individual, sifting through experiences intelligently, becoming aware of how they impact our behavior, being reasonable in making decisions, being responsible for the decisions made, and being in love with God and God's creation (p. 20).

Entering into a deeper relationship with God is paramount in this discernment journey; demonstrating and extending this love to God's creation—community members, people we serve in ministry, the entire God's people, and the planet Earth—is the ultimate goal of loving God. Matthew 25:40 explains: And the king will answer them, "Truly I tell you, whatever you did to one of the least of my brethren, you did it to me." This love must be encompassing, both within the religious community and outside of it.

The Importance of Formation of Formators:

Every formator needs to be adequately trained for formation ministry to guide formees in initial formation. Gitau (2016, p.134) and O'Reilly (2013, p.125) emphasize the need for appropriate preparation of a formator since a formator is involved in the personal life of those who are being formed. It is imperative that formators are well-trained for the ministry of formation. Such preparation would assist them in expanding their self-knowledge and discerning the inner dispositions and attitudes of those in formation to avoid causing harm to the formees.

Maganya (2016), an African priest, also agreed that formation has to be holistic and cater to the psychological, spiritual, theological, moral, anthropological, and sexual dimensions of human development. Thus, well-trained personnel are needed in formation houses (p. 143). Granted, some formators are trained, but they may still lack the necessary skills for the ministry of formation. It is crucial to have well-trained formators, as many candidates seeking to join religious life come from dysfunctional and broken homes, as explained above. Many of them are wounded from adverse childhood experiences, and they need healing before the formation process can transform them.

A wise saying attributed to James Baldwin explicates that it is "not everything that is faced can be changed, but nothing can be changed until it is faced." When these wounds are not adequately addressed in therapy, they continue to impact the behavior of the religious person. Complete healing will not happen miraculously. However, being aware of the underlying cause of the behavior can lead to change through the grace of God. Therefore, the energy could be focused on building the new, rather than fighting the old, which is the secret of change, says Socrates.

Ultimately, there is a need to integrate the formees' broken past history into their beautiful call to religious life through an integrated formation process. And this is only possible through a well-trained formator and the desire for therapy. Maganya explained that it is not enough to appoint persons to formation ministry because they are available, or because they are best-behaved people, bright, or intelligent since formees to religious life deserve well-trained formators who can do exegesis of their lives in all honesty and somehow have integrated their weaknesses and their strengths in a balanced manner (p. 145).

Sometimes, when formators are not properly trained, it can lead to crises for both the individual seeking guidance and the formator providing inadequate and half-baked formation procedures. When formators are not trained, they will be battling with their insecurity, and may induce the candidates to conform to their wishes. When this is the case, transformation and internalization of the values of formation will never take place. As such, formators can be caught up in blurred relationships with the formees, leading to favoritism and co-dependent relationships with the formees (Gitau, p.137).

Ezeani (2017) illumines that when formators are not well trained, their sense of self-confidence and self-esteem might not be solid, and they may feel threatened by a formee who takes a stand on issues that do not agree with the formator's position. She continues to say that at times when this happens, various measures are employed to punish the formee, and in extreme cases, the individual is expelled from the formation house (p. 45).

Granted, there are instances of resistance to the formation process when it is right to discontinue the person who does not fit into religious life (Pope Francis address to formators in Rome, April 2015). When a formator is not properly trained, they inadvertently create a system where success in religious life is based on how much the person being formed is willing to follow the formator's rules. In such cases, the religious individual may end up taking their perpetual vows without going through the necessary growth and healing that should occur during the formation process.

The Role of Community of Religious Persons:

Canon Law defines community life as living a fraternal life in common which arises from hearts animated by charity. It underlines "communion of life" and interpersonal relationships, which consist of living in one's own lawfully constituted religious house and living together in fidelity to the same norms and way of life of the congregation, and taking part in common acts and services (Can. 12-14). Thus, gathered in their various communities, religious persons point out to all the baptized faithful and to all people how to use earthly goods through the vow of poverty, the deeper meaning of love through the vow of chastity, and the gift of freedom through the vow of obedience.

Religious persons live in communities. These are homes modeled after the way of life of the disciples of Jesus who, with one mind and heart, lived together, prayed together, and shared everything in common (Acts. 2:44; 4:32). In the same way, religious persons live together in a house designed for it; they pray together, socialize and enjoy table fellowship together, and share all they have in common.

In many communities, members are happy, supportive, hospitable, and kind to one another. In these communities, the philosophy of *Ubuntu* is practiced. *Ubuntu* is a Zulu word translated as "I am because we are." The Ubuntu philosophy emphasizes that individuals are not isolated but are part of a larger community. It promotes respect for the dignity of every person. This community thrives on principles of justice, fairness, hospitality, and love. Desmond Tutu (2008) explained: "Ubuntu speaks particularly about the fact that you can't exist as a human being in isolation. It speaks about our interconnectedness. You can't be human all by yourself." Just as God exists in a relational nature as a Triune God, He also created us to be in a relationship with one another.

The Scripture says "Behold, how good and how pleasant it is for brothers and sisters to dwell together in unity! (Psalm 133:1). In another place, it says: "Above all, maintain constant love for one another, for love covers a multitude of sins. Be hospitable to one another without complaining. Like good stewards of the manifold grace of God, serve one another with whatever gift each of you has received (1 Peter 4:8-10). These scripture passages reflect the philosophy of *Ubuntu*, where community members are hospitable, and no one feels threatened by the blessings of other's gifts.

At times, the beautiful philosophy of Ubuntu is overshadowed by human frailty. Pope Francis once said: "Community Life is very important, although it is not a paradise; rather, it's a purgatory" (Pope Francis addresses seminarians from the Pontifical Roman universities on May 12, 2014). We encounter various challenges, including childhood wounds, personality clashes, addiction to social media, triangulation, boundary issues, misunderstandings, ineffective communication, and the difficulties associated with intercultural and intergenerational living. Additionally, we face issues related to ethnocentrism, microaggression, prejudice, unforgiveness, bitterness, individualism, and a lack of appropriate self-care. At times, we struggle to balance our ministry responsibilities with our prayer life. All these challenges can be gracefully embraced when we adhere to the culture of encounter.

Pope Francis calls us to the culture of encounter. He says: "The word, "encounter," is very important. Why? Because faith is an encounter with Jesus, and we must do what Jesus does: encounter others. With our faith, we must create a "culture of encounter," a culture of friendship." The culture of encounter reminds me of another South African concept, *Sawubona. Sawubona* is the most common greeting in the Zulu language. It literally means, "I see you, you are important to me, and I value you." It acknowledges the other person and accepts them as they are, with their virtues and flaws. This encounter promotes the spirit of the synodal walk, where community members are valued, and all are welcomed! It promotes a culture of respect, forgiveness, empathy, collaboration, acceptance, non-violent communication, and equity.

In his recent encyclical on the Human and Divine Love of the Heart of Jesus Christ, Pope Francis explains: "It is only by starting from the heart that our communities will succeed in uniting and reconciling differing minds and wills, so that the Spirit can guide us in unity as brothers and sisters. Reconciliation and peace are also born of the heart. The heart of Christ is "ecstasy," openness, gift, and encounter. In that heart, we learn to relate to one another in wholesome and happy ways, and to build up in this world God's kingdom of love and justice. Our hearts, united with the heart of Christ, are capable of working this social miracle" (Dilexit nos, 2024, # 28). We have to start from the Heart of Jesus which is overflowing with compassion. The culture of encounter helps us find grace in community living. Our communities should be filled with joy and hope because spending time with joyful and optimistic people can be a lot of fun. Pope Francis, in his Apostolic Letter to all Consecrated People, On the Occasion of the Year of Consecrated Life in 2014, encouraged all consecrated people to look to the past with gratitude, live the present with passion, and embrace the future with hope.

These are the values that should set us apart as consecrated persons. The radical life that Jesus Christ initiated is a countercultural life of simplicity of heart and poverty of spirit. Jesus, who is the Head of the Body, the Church, calls us into union with him, and this union is not devoid of suffering. Christ's union with a religious person is so intimate that, as a consequence, a religious cannot but seek to reflect in his/her person the light of Christ and cause his features to shine forth holiness, charity, and grace (*Lumen Gentium*, # 44, 46). In fact, religious individuals live out their consecration only if they remain connected with Christ and are identified with him in his suffering and in his glory. Thus, religious persons vow to Christ with a preferential love, even to the point of sacrificing certain authentic human values, such as spousal and parental love, the possession of goods, and independent decision-making. It is in the communities that a religious person lives out this vowed life of chastity, poverty, and obedience.

The call to religious life and the response to this call are gifts from God for a specific mission in the Church and in the world. Therefore, when an individual desires to respond to this call but has been affected by adverse childhood experiences, it significantly impacts their confidence in themselves, in others, and in the world. Consequently, it affects the adult's relationships with self, with community members, with the environment, and with God.

Having introduced the work and who a religious person is, the reflective questions that guided this work include: In what ways do childhood experiences affect the development of faith in religious individuals? What role do parental care and religiosity play in the faith development of adult women and men? How do childhood experiences influence the way religious individuals relate with their community members, even after years of religious formation? What steps can religious institutes take to address the impact of adverse childhood experiences on their members?

In responding to these questions, chapter two explores the meaning and impacts of childhood experiences through Erik Erikson's psychosocial theory of human development. This helps to better understand the impact of childhood experiences on adult life. Chapter three discusses faith development in children using James Fowler's faith development theory. It also explores the impact of parental religiosity on a child's religious development and its continuity into adulthood. Chapter four reflects and analyses the faith development and childhood experiences of some men and women religious and how these experiences impact their religious commitments. Chapter five explains the meaning and process of psychotherapy, focusing on major theories in psychology. It emphasizes cognitive behavioral therapy and psychospiritual therapy and their application in the healing process of wounded individuals. Chapter six summarizes the work and provides recommendations to assist congregations in their formation process and aid religious individuals in living a fulfilled life. The epilogue concludes this work.

It is my hope that this work will enhance people's lives in the following ways:

Religious individuals may find it helpful to understand how their childhood experiences influence their religious life. Seeking help to address any related issues and responding more generously to the values they are receiving can lead to a healthier religious life, whether they are in initial or ongoing formation.

The formators, who accompany individuals in their formation journey, can gain a better understanding of the formees and how their childhood experiences influenced their faith development. As a result, they can use methods that address these issues for a more effective formative process and psychological maturity.

The Major Superiors, who make deliberative/definitive decisions about the vocation of the religious persons, may assist the formators in decision-making and offer guidance and advice on how to facilitate growth and development opportunities for religious individuals.

Individuals who are not religious can benefit from this work by gaining insights into how their history of maltreatment, neglect, care, and love has impacted their lives and values as adults. They can seek help to cope well with life challenges and daily stresses.

Drawing from ongoing discussions and research on how childhood experiences impact adult life, and utilizing the theories of psychosocial development by Erik Erikson and the faith development theory by James Fowler, this work contributes to the conversation.

It reflects on how to bridge the gap between psychology and spirituality, including religion, which is increasingly being examined in relation to psychological adjustment. Childhood experiences in connection with faith development are important in psychology for the formation program of religious individuals.

The book titled "*Influence of Childhood Experiences on Faith Development: A Journey Toward Wholeness*" was very helpful in shedding light on the influence of childhood experiences on the development of faith in religious individuals. It explores ways to support and participate in a transformative formative process. The intention of this work is not to "wash the dirty linens of religious persons in public," but it is intended to help those who are wounded to start the journey toward wholeness.

This work was possible through the semi-structured interview of sampled eighty religious men and women who have made their vows: religious in annual (temporal) vows as well as those in perpetual vows. A semi-structured interview is a research method in which the interviewer does not strictly follow a formalized list of questions in data collection, but rather a flexible open-ended and close-ended questions. The writer interviewed forty consecrated men and forty consecrated women, from over 60 different congregations and across cultures. Some participants chose not to have their stories included in this book, and the writer respected their decision. Others agreed to have their stories published as long as their names and congregations remained confidential. Consequently, the author used stories from some participants with their consent while ensuring their personal information remained confidential. Having introduced the work, chapter two will delve into Erik Erikson's theory to explore the impact of childhood experiences on an adult's life.

CHAPTER TWO

Childhood Experiences: Meaning and Influence on Adults

"Indeed, the good of the family is decisive for the future of the world and of the Church."

—Pope Francis (Amoris Laetitia)

Introduction

Every child is nurtured first by the family and then by the environment—Parents, siblings, close relatives, teachers, peer groups, religious figures, elders in the community, media, etc. The family is the basic unit where a child starts feeling the impact of love, trust, and concern. Through breastfeeding, a smile, and the touch of the mother, the child begins to interact with the mother. I watched a short YouTube clip by Dr. Edward Tronick, an American Developmental Psychologist, on what the still face of a mother does to the baby. His experiment proved that infant babies are extremely responsive to the emotions and reactivity of the world around them and that infants could engage in social interaction. In other words, a child is happy and responds with a playful attitude when the mother is smiling. But when the mother is on the phone or has a still face, the baby tries to get her attention. When this attention is not responded to by the mother, the baby reacts negatively and cries.

Winnicott (1967) explained it well: A mother's love displayed through smile, touch, and playful gestures does, in fact, give the baby a sense of trust and confidence (p. 372). The mother's smile and touch communicate love and acceptance, while her still face communicates rejection.

This confirmed my experience one Sunday morning during Mass. A mother sitting on a pew in front of me was holding her baby boy, and the boy was facing me. I thought to myself, "Let me try something here." I smiled at the baby to get his attention. He smiled back and clapped his hands in a happy gesture. This happened several times at the beginning of the Mass. During the homily, I tried to concentrate, but the baby kept smiling and gesturing at me to interact. At this point, I wasn't returning his smile. This made him angry, and he started making loud attention-seeking noises. When I finally smiled back, he gave me a big smile and stopped the noise. However, his behavior was becoming a distraction, and the people around me were getting distracted. During the Eucharistic prayer, I closed my eyes so as not to look at him. Despite his attempts to get my attention, I ignored him. Eventually, he started crying, and his mother had to take him out of the church. The joy, love, and acceptance that I was giving to the baby were not consistent, which made him angry and led to him expressing his emotions by crying.

From contact with people around and from their significant others, children start noticing and learning that a smile is a sign of acceptance and love, while an unhappy facial expression is a sign of rejection. Consequently, the child develops trust in the significant others if the love the baby is receiving is consistent and reliable. Basically, family is an important unit and a system that facilitates how interactions and developmental relationships are formed and sustained over time.

Parental care is the time and resources the significant other dedicates to caring for the child. In other words, it is the process of promoting and supporting the physical, biological, spiritual, emotional, psychological, social, financial, and intellectual development of a child from infancy to young adulthood. Sometimes, a child is left with one of the parents, the older siblings, a nanny, house help, grandparents, step-parents, orphanage centers, schools, or day-care centers because the parents are absent or because they are career-oriented. At this early stage, the child inculcates all kinds of behaviors. Indeed, one of the fortunate things that can happen to a person in life is to have a loving and caring childhood experience. When a mother's smile is replaced by a consistently still or angry expression, when a child experiences physical abuse, neglect, or lack of attention, the child unconsciously internalizes feelings of rejection and insecurity, believing that, 'I am not loved or wanted.'

Childhood experiences can be positive or negative. A positive childhood experience is when a child receives consistent love, care, and support, which leads to trust, security, and the ability to love and to be loved (Erikson, 1950). When a child receives attention from parents, she/he creatively expresses the same acquired care to her/his doll or pet. For example, female children play motherhood with their toys by bathing, feeding, and embracing them.

On the other hand, childhood experiences of mistreatment in the form of rejection, neglect, lack of attention, corporal punishment, verbal abuse, name-calling, physical abuse, emotional abuse, sexual abuse, or consistent negative criticism can lead to mistrust, shame, insecurity, inferiority complex, inability to love and to feel loved, as well as low self-confidence. Sacks, Murphy, and Moore (2014) explain that "adverse childhood experiences are potentially traumatic events that can have negative and lasting effects on the health and well-being of the individual. These experiences range from physical, emotional, or sexual abuse to parental divorce or the incarceration of a parent or guardian" (p. 1). A child can face developmental impairment during the early stages of life when the baby faces emotional starvation and unconsciously becomes a partner in the family tragedy caused by parental oppression, rejection, and neglect (Adelson and Shapiro, 1987, P. 102). The parents also could be burdened by their own childhood experiences, which were never dealt with, and this could be the experiences of the past three or four generations. Thus, babies become victims of the oppressive past of their parents from the moment they enter the womb.

Literature on Childhood Experiences and Impacts on Adults:

Parental strategies in raising children have a significant impact on their developmental outcomes. It is expected that negative parenting behaviors, such as strictness, neglect, excessive control, punishment, and lack of support, can lead to behavioral problems in children, including emotional issues and misconduct. The findings of a number of studies reveal an association between the quality of parenting styles and children's behavioral problems (Anthony et al., 2005; Aunola & Kurmi, 2005; Chang, Schwartz, Dodge, & McBride-Chang, 2003; Mulvaney & Mebert, 2007; Stevens, Vollebergh, Pels, & Crijnen, 2007). More specifically, Barnes and Farrell (1992) found that parenting styles were significant predictors of behavioral problems, suggesting that positive parenting techniques such as a high level of parental support and monitoring tended to have children who were less likely to exhibit drinking problems, drug use, misconduct at school and deviant behavior in general (Sangawi, Adams, & Reissland 2015, p. 171).

The findings of the study carried out by Loken and Reigstad (2012) show that experiences of maltreatment during childhood impair one's interpersonal functioning later in life. They discovered that some of the long-term consequences suffered by adults who are victims of abuse or neglect are trust issues, anger, relational imbalances, low self-esteem, inappropriate coping skills (e.g., substance abuse), a feeling of powerlessness, internalization of aggression, depression, and anxiety (p. 39). In her research work, Vandervender (2014), discovered that individuals with a history of childhood maltreatment report lower levels of self-esteem than their non-maltreated counterparts (p. 2). Mvungu (2014) also ascertains that family characteristics such as poor parental supervision, parental violence, and abuse, low parental involvement with the child, parental aggression, including erratic or harsh parental discipline, a difficult economy, as well as antisocial parents have been found to greatly contribute to behavior maladjustment in children. These abuses, in the form of physical or emotional, can have long-term consequences that endure into an individual's adult life, influencing the way individuals view and interact with their world, system of belief, and practices.

Physical violence is the use of physical force such as kicking, slapping, punching, hair-pulling, stabbing, choking, pushing, beating, and biting to inflict harm on an individual. Emotional or psychological abuse is in the form of negative criticism, social isolation, verbal assault, intimidation, humiliation, name-calling, shaming, or harming self-worth in order to put someone down and so diminish the sense of identity, dignity, and self-pride (Ogbuji, 2015, p. 38).

Emotional abuse is an attempt to control, in just the same way that physical abuse is an attempt to control another person. The only difference is that the emotional abuser does not use physical violence such as hitting, kicking, pinching, grabbing, pushing, or other physical forms of harm. Rather, the perpetrator of emotional abuse uses verbal attack as his/her weapon of choice. Child neglect is a form of child abuse and is a deficit in meeting a child's basic needs, such as love, clothing, food, shelter, and adequate care, including the failure to provide adequate health care.

Glaser, (2002) lists the following categories of neglect that affect behavior: emotional unavailability, unresponsiveness, and neglect; negative attributions and misattributions to a child; developmentally inappropriate or inconsistent interactions with a child, failure to recognize or acknowledge a child's individuality and psychological bond; and the failure to promote a child's social adaptation. Obviously, experiencing care or neglect from a significant other can lead to different behaviors, thoughts, or feelings. When children are left unsupervised, they may make immature decisions.

At the same time, over-pampering the child can also lead to selfishness and irresponsible behavior.

A story is told of two neighbors who had planted identical saplings on their respective sides of the compound wall. One was a retired elderly man, and the other was a young techie (An expert in technology). The young guy supplies his plant with abundant water and high-quality manure, while the retired man gives his plant a small quantity of water and small manure. The techie's sapling grew into a lush, green, leafy, and robust plant; the retired man's plant, however, was much more luxuriant than his neighbor's. One night, there was a heavy rain with gusty wind. The next morning, both came out to see the fate of their plants. To the techie's surprise, his plant has been uprooted, while his neighbors' plant is unharmed. The young man turned to his neighbor and asked: "Why was my plant uprooted by the rains despite such good care, whereas yours stayed firm and strong despite little care?" The old man responded: "Look, young man, you supplied everything that the plant would need in abundance. Since the plant did not have to do anything on its own to search for what it needed, the roots of your plants have not gone deep down. I only provided enough to keep my plant alive. As a result, its roots had to grow deep into the ground to find more of what it needed. Your plants had shallow roots and were easily affected by rain and wind. In contrast, my plants had deep roots and could easily withstand nature's forces."

This story is similar to the parental care of children. Sometimes, parents are so possessive and overprotective of their children that they end up over-pampering their children, not giving them the space, the opportunity, and the impetus to grow and become responsible. Some parents provide their children with whatever they ask for: a bike, laptop, phone, toys of every kind, etc., in order for the child to be happy. But do these things bring happiness? These can rather lead to the ill effects of being over-indulged in material things, which may consequently lead to the desire for more things.

Children from this kind of background may develop the habit of becoming accustomed to a materialistic attitude and the need to acquire goods even higher than what they can afford as adults. When this is the case, children may develop the habit of affluence, not by working for it, sacrificing, or doing their best, but by whining, demanding, or manipulating attitudes, even as adults, in order to get what they want. This can pass from one generation to the next.

Caring for children is like caring for a plant. Underdoing it will cause the plant to die and overdoing it will weaken the plant. Children need attention, protection, direction, and affection. They deserve to learn the importance of putting effort into their creativity, rather than expecting things to come easily. Providing them with the right balance of care, guidance, and support will help children mature into responsible adults who will reap the rewards of wisdom and maturity.

This is in line with Erikson's theory that consistent love and support develop a sense of security and trust in a child. However, to understand the effects of childhood experiences on an individual, this work will turn to the theory of Erik Homburger Erikson's psychosocial theory of human development, focusing only on the first four stages.

Psychosocial Theory of Human Development

Erik Homburger Erikson (1902-94) was born in Frankfurt, Germany, on June 15th, 1902, to a young Jewish woman, Karla Abrahamsen. There is a little mystery about his heritage: His biological father was an unnamed Danish man who abandoned Erik's mother before he was born. His mother, Karla, raised him alone for the first three years of his life. She then married Dr. Theodor Homberger, who was Erik's pediatrician, and they moved to Karlsruhe in Southern Germany (Boerce, 2006, p. 5).

A degree of uncertainty about personal identity and direction apparently characterized Erik's childhood and early adult years - not surprisingly given his circumstances - which reflected and perhaps helped inspire his life and work. During his childhood, and his early adulthood, he was Erik Homberger, and his parents kept the details of his birth a secret. At temple school, the kids teased him for being Nordic; at grammar school, they teased him for being Jewish. (Boerce, p. 5).

After graduating from high school, Erik focused on becoming an artist. When not taking art classes, he wandered around Europe, visiting museums and sleeping under bridges. He was living the life of a carefree rebel. When he was 25, his friend Peter Blos – a fellow artist and later, psychoanalyst – suggested that he apply for a teaching position at an experimental school for American students run by Dorothy Burlingham, a friend of Anna Freud. Besides teaching art, he gathered a certificate in Montessori education and one from the Vienna Psychoanalytic Society. He was psychoanalyzed by Anna Freud herself.

While at the school, he met Joan Serson, a Canadian dance teacher. They went on to have three children, one of whom became a sociologist. With the Nazis coming into power, they left Vienna, first for Copenhagen, then to Boston. Erikson was offered a position at the Harvard Medical School, and he practiced child psychoanalysis privately. He later taught at Yale, and later still at the University of California at Berkeley. It was during this period of time that he did his famous studies of modern life among the Native Indians. Erik later changed his surname, seemingly on becoming an American citizen. No one seems to know where he got the name from (Boerce, 2006, p. 5).

Erik Erikson's theory of psychosocial development is an eight-stage theory that describes how personality develops and changes throughout the course of the entire lifespan. As each person progresses through life, from infancy up until death, they confront different challenges that can either be mastered or that can lead to crises (Scheck, 2005, p. 4). While each stage builds on the experiences of earlier stages, Erikson didn't believe that mastering each stage was necessary in order to move on to the next. Like other stage theorists, Erikson believed that these stages occurred in a predetermined order, a concept known as the epigenetic principle (Erikson, 1959).

The psychosocial theory explains that the experience of consistent affection and love helps a child from 0-4 years to develop trust in his parents and the people around him and to develop autonomy. A child gradually learns to play with other children, to take initiative, and to learn appropriate gender roles and relationships with age mates of both sexes. The child learns to accept physical changes and appearances of the body, learns to be at ease with the opposite sex, and learns the ability to make decisions. The child's ego develops as it successfully resolves crises that are distinctly social in nature (McLeod, 2013).

According to Schultz and Schultz (2009), the developed ego preserves identity through:

1. Individuality: a conscious sense of uniqueness and existence as a separate distinct entity;
2. Wholeness and synthesis: a sense of inner wholeness and indivisibility resulting from unconscious synthesizing operations of the ego;
3. Sameness and continuity: a feeling that one's life is consistent and is headed in a meaningful direction;
4. Social solidarity: a sense of inner solidarity with group values and a feeling of social support and validation.

Thus, a well-developed ego manifests in trust for self and significant others, developing a sense of identity in society, and helping the next generation prepare for the future (McLeod, 2013). This is possible because of the recognition and care of the child from the significant others who are important to the child. However, when there are environmental contradictions, the child feels lost and may experience crises during the developmental stages.

Like Freud, Erikson assumes that a crisis occurs at each stage of development. Erikson believes that these crises must be faced before advancing to subsequent stages (Charles, Reynolds, & Gatz, 2001). For Erikson, these crises are psychosocial because they involve the individual's psychological needs. The crises are rather a state through which constructive resolution leads to further development. Thus, the successful handling of each phase is important for the next phase. In his view, human development is a process alternating between phases, crises, and the new balance to reach an increasingly mature stage (Scheck, p. 4). Failure to successfully complete a stage can result in a reduced ability to complete further stages and, therefore, an unhealthier personality and low sense of self. These stages, however, can be resolved successfully at a later time (McLeod, 2013). As individuals continue to age, they will progress through the stages regardless of whether or not the conflicts have been resolved because each stage builds upon another (Dunkel & Sefcek, 2009).

The stages Erikson proposes include trust versus mistrust, autonomy vs. shame/doubt, initiative vs. guilt, industry vs. inferiority, identity vs. role confusion, intimacy vs. isolation, generativity vs. stagnation, and integrity vs. despair (as cited in Logan, 1986). Like Sigmund Freud's theory of psychosexual development, Erikson's developmental stages are closely tied to ages in which people are expected to experience crises and development.

Below is the psychosocial development according to Erikson (McLeod, 2013):

Stage	Psychosocial Crisis	Basic Virtue	Age
1	Trust vs. mistrust	Hope	Infancy (o to1 ½)
2	Autonomy vs. shame	Will	Early Childhood (1 ½ to3)
3	Initiative vs. guilt	Purpose	Play Age (3 to 5)
4	Industry vs. inferiority	Competency	School Age (5 to 12)
5	Ego identity vs. Role Confusion	Fidelity	Adolescence (12 to 18)
6	Intimacy vs. isolation	Love	Young Adult (18 to 40)
7	Generativity vs. stagnation	Care	Adult hood(40 to 65)
8	Ego integrity vs. despair	Wisdom	Maturity (65+)

Table 1: The summary of the stages of psychosocial development

This work will now concentrate on the first four stages of psychosocial development:

1. Trust vs. Mistrust: Erikson's first psychosocial crisis occurs during the first year. The crisis is one of trust versus mistrust. During this stage, the infant is uncertain about the world in which they live. To resolve these feelings of uncertainty the infant looks toward their primary caregiver for stability and consistency of care. If the care the infant receives is consistent, predictable, and reliable, they will develop a sense of trust which they will carry with them to other relationships, and they will be able to feel secure even when threatened. Thus, success in this stage leads to hope. On the other hand, when the care has been harsh or inconsistent, unpredictable and unreliable, then the infant will develop a sense of mistrust and will not have confidence in the world around them or in their abilities to influence events (McLeod, 2013).

2. Autonomy vs. Shame & Doubt: Autonomy means self-reliance. This is independence of thought and a basic confidence to think and act for oneself. Shame and doubt obviously inhibit self-expression and developing one's own ideas, opinions and sense of self. At this stage, the child is developing physically and becoming more mobile. Between the ages of 18 months and three years, children begin to assert their independence, by walking away from their mother, picking which toy to play with, and making choices about what they like to wear, or to eat, etc. When children are criticized, overly controlled, or not given the opportunity to assert themselves, they start feeling inadequate in their ability to survive. As a result, they may become overly dependent on others, lack self-esteem, and feel a sense of shame or doubt in their own abilities (McLeod, 2013).

3. Initiative vs. Guilt: Initiative is the capability to devise actions or projects, and a confidence and belief to do so, even with a risk of failure or making mistakes. Guilt is the feeling that it is wrong or inappropriate to instigate something of one's own design. Suppressing adventure and experimentation, or preventing young children from doing things for themselves, will hinder the development of confidence to initiate. Instead, it can instill an unhelpful fear of being wrong or disapproved of. Therefore, it is the responsibility of parents to provide children with a safe environment that allows for trial and error, while minimizing criticism and scolding. This will give the child the freedom for adventure and discovery, and help them develop self-confidence.

4. Industry vs. Inferiority: Industry here refers to purposeful or meaningful activity. It is the development of competence and skills where children learn to read and write, to do sums, and to do things on their own. During this stage, teachers play a crucial role in a child's life by teaching them specific skills. At this point, the child's peer group becomes increasingly important and serves as a major source of their self-esteem. When children are supported and rewarded for their efforts, they develop a sense of industry and confidence in their ability to achieve goals. However, if their initiative is not encouraged and is instead restricted by parents or teachers, the child may start to feel inferior, doubting their own abilities, and consequently may not reach their full potential.

These stages, especially from birth to 5 years, are the cornerstone of a vital personality (Scheck, 2005, p. 5). Here, the social reference person is the significant others, especially the parents who, through offering their love, care, and breasts through the mother, meet the basic needs of eating, oral satisfaction, smiling, playful gestures, security, the potential of trial and error that makes for creativity, and the ability to trust. Parents are encouraged to avoid severe reprimanding and punishment that might send a signal of hatred, but to provide care the child can rely on in order to develop trust. Trust here means an essential trustfulness in others as well as a fundamental sense of one's own trustworthiness, sense of identity, and sense of being oneself (Scheck, p. 5).

During the first stage of psychosocial development, infants are uncertain about the world in which they live. To resolve these feelings of uncertainty, the infants look toward their primary caregiver for stability, love, and consistency of care. If the care the infants receive is consistent, predictable, and reliable, they will develop a sense of trust, which they will carry with them to other relationships, and they will feel secure even when threatened. However, if the care has been harsh or inconsistent, unkind, unpredictable, and unreliable, then the infants will develop a sense of mistrust, and they will not have confidence in the world around them or in their abilities to influence events (McLeod, 2013). This basic trust in oneself and others will form the basis for any later development. What is the fate of a child whose primary caregiver is abusive?

The Kenya *Daily Nation,* on March 27, 2017, reported a pathetic story of how a 12-year-old Angela was repeatedly defiled by her father from a tender age. During the day when his wife was away working as a waitress, the man would send his sons to the shop so that he could be left alone to defile his daughter. However, one fateful afternoon, he did not notice that the children had come back, and they watched as their father shamelessly violated their sister. When his wife confronted him about the incident, he rained blows on her. Unperturbed, the woman reported the beating and the defilement of her daughter to the police. However, her relatives condemned her for reporting the case and urged her to settle the matter out of court. Angela had trust in her father and thought that she was loved by her father, only to realize that the father was sexually abusing her. She submitted to this abuse since she was lavished with gifts—the innocence and total trust of a child (Okeyo, 2017).

One of the participants during the interview was raped by her drunk father when she was very young. She explained: "The experience of being raped has caused me to dislike and distrust my father. I also feel insecure, lonely, and empty inside."

These victims of sexual abuse might suffer insecurity and mistrust even as adults because their initial child-like trust has been affected and wounded by abuse from the significant other. Erikson theory clearly explains that the basic trust or mistrust is dependent on parenting and the social environment of a child from as early as infancy.

Apparently, a child also needs a variation in the response he or she receives from adults in order to realize they are separate humans and to move toward learning how to solve problems, handle stress, and be independent. Thus, some stress is part of healthy development. It's only when the stress response is triggered too often that the physiological reactions of the body can become a threat to brain development. Gilmore and Meersand (2014) put it well:

> As toddlers develop awareness of their own and their mothers' separate and distinct bodies and minds, they simultaneously grapple with a new set of cultural requirements. In infancy, the baby's limited motor, cognitive, and communicative capacities necessitated nearly total dependence on parents. However, as the child acquires language and rudimentary self-restraint, crawling, walking, etc., the 2-or 3-year-old child begins controlling bowel and bladder urges. (p.46)

At this time, the child needs support to deal with the stress of growing up and the challenges of trying to discover who they are. Evidently, children do not need a "perfect childhood." However, they need healthy social connections, routines, play, good role models from the caregiver, and affection and acceptance, which may lead to their ability to develop trust and faith in themselves and others.

Therefore, for a child to grow up into an adult who can confidently form healthy relationships with others, he needs a strong and reliable bond with a caregiver for the first few years of their life. This means that when a child cries, gestures, or otherwise tries to express a need, an adult responds in an appropriate and caring way. Perhaps to pick the child up and hold the child lovingly, to speak, and to console the child in order for the child to feel safe. In this way, trust is developed, especially when love, affirmation, care, guidance, support, and acceptance are consistent. Consequently, the child develops a sense of security, trust in self and others, ability to take roles, effective coping skills, good self-concept, creative thinking, and confidence in the significant other and in self-worth. When children are raised in a healthy environment, they are far more likely to grow into high-functioning adults with good confidence and self-worth, who have constructive coping strategies in difficult times.

Certainly, each time a positive interaction takes place between a child and an adult, neural connections are built (Cabral, 2017). Neural connections form throughout our lives. Although the bulk of the development of the brain happens while in the womb, our brain continues to grow and build itself. Scientists cannot say exactly what percentage of our brain is developed by what age; but they are sure that childhood is a crucial period of growth. It is estimated that in the first few years of life, our brain forms from 700 to 1,000 neural connections every second. And these connections form the foundation for further brain development (Cabral, 2017). The interaction of a child and the significant other is thus important, not only for psychological development as an infant but also for the healthy development of a child's brain.

When healthy interactions do not take place or if the significant other's care is unreliable, these neural connections or pathways may not form as strongly as it is supposed to. Consequently, mental and emotional health may be impaired as an adult. Any kind of abuse–physical abuse, sexual abuse, or emotional abuse–is very traumatic for a child and will affect brain development. Science now shows that childhood trauma actually affects our brains (Cabral, 2017). If childhood negative experiences could affect the brain, subsequently, it could affect an adult's faith or religious development. The next chapter will explicate in detail the faith development theory and the childhood experiences that impact religious development.

CHAPTER THREE

Faith Development in Early Childhood

"Faith is taking the first step even when you don't see the whole staircase."

—Martin Luther King, Jr.

Introduction

This chapter introduces faith development theory and how a child develops values and trust in self and others. It also explains how parental religiosity influences the religious development of a child. Our values are nurtured and shaped during childhood by the influence of our primary caregiver and can be either positive or negative. They greatly impact our thoughts, behaviors, and emotions. Our values are what we consider important in our actions and thoughts towards ourselves and others, and they influence our faith in ourselves, others, and the Divine.

Faith development is the process of developing, through experiences, a general feeling about self-worth, self-value, self-belief, self-identity, and self-efficacy in relation to others and God (Fowler, 1981, p. 31). An individual's faith development reflects a "meaning-making" process in which individuals seek to understand their own lives and values as well as God's story as told by parents and significant others.

Extensive research has explored various themes related to development theory, from humanism to cognitivism, within the field of psychology. An American theologian, James W. Fowler's Stages of Faith Development (1981), is an excellent example of converging various developmental theories and models into a single theoretical paradigm of faith. It was his experiences of listening to people's spiritual stories that led Fowler to attempt an empirically founded developmental theory called faith development theory (Fowler, 2004).

The theory of faith development is presented in relation to Jean Piaget's theory of cognitive development, Erik Erikson's theory of psychosocial development, and Laurence Kohlberg's theory of moral development (Moore, 2016, P. 2). Fowler situates faith development stages within these developmental models, suggesting that, as children mature, they have an increased ability to become more aware and engaged with their faith. Through nurturing from the environment and significant others, children gradually develop the capacity to attach meaning and value to events and circumstances. This meaning and value guide their decisions, their views about life, and how they relate with people around them.

Faith Development

Faith, in this work, is the value and trust a child develops in the significant other at the tender age, which leads to finding meaning in life, while developing self-confidence, self-value, and trust. According to Fowler, faith is a relationship because it binds people together with others who share their commitments; it is also the relationship that ultimately concerns human beings (Fowler, 1981, p.

18). There are different dimensions of faith: faith in self, in nature, in others, in religion, in material things, in a spouse, in political power, in money, etc., and ultimately faith in God, which is a divine gift and which develops with personal encounter or experience with God. This is true because one can have knowledge of God without faith in God. Coyle (2011) explains that faith describes the underlying meaning-making process used by all people regardless of their beliefs. It occurs as individuals place personal trust and loyalty in one or more "centers of value" such as religion, God, family, friends, spouses, money, power, and so on (Fowler, 1991). Where we place our trust is sometimes determined by the experiences that nurtured who we are.

Fowler stated further that faith and religion are not synonymous and should not be considered as such, as faith is defined as "a generic feature of the human struggle to find and maintain meaning" (Fowler, 1981, p. 91). However, that meaning does not necessarily have to be found through religion. Questions regarding faith that people ask themselves revolve around what gives their life meaning, love, and purpose, as well as what their hopes for themselves and their loved ones are, among many others (Fowler, 1981). Thus, faith becomes a prerequisite for hope and love, "Now these three remain—faith, hope, and love... (1 Corinthians 13:13). When trust or faith develops, hope and love for self and others follow naturally. This is true because if one believes in self and in one's capability to achieve greater objectives, then it leads to a better attitude and habit, which consequently leads to the hope that one can achieve success, then the love of self and others naturally follows. Hence, faith comprises the way individuals evolve and the ways they experience themselves, others, and the world.

Faith, in this case, is in its verb form and is used generically. It is a universal element of the human condition in that everyone believes in something or someone, which brings order and coherence to life (Zinnbauer & Pargament, 2005). Consequently, religious faith is only one aspect of human faith, which is faith directed to religious things or God.

The faith development model focuses on the psychological factors that facilitate the operation of faith and does not address any specific content of faith, values, and beliefs of a particular religion. Thus, an individual's faith is understood as having at its core a disposition or stance, attitudes, values, beliefs, and practices that "animate people's lives" and inform their behavior (Streib & Hood, 2011). The psychological processes of faith are rooted in a person's ability to reason logically, take on societal roles, demonstrate honesty, make moral judgments, show social awareness, maintain control and cope with life's challenges, and function effectively in society.

There are many factors that influence faith development, which can be positive or negative, and the most important are environmental and spiritual experiences as well as social, religious, cultural, educational, and psychological factors. These are in the form of the caregiver's nurturing and supporting love, parental religious influence, peer group influence, community influence, academic influence, professional/occupational influence, and ultimately, the encounter with the Divine or the experience of God. Other factors that can impact faith are the zeal to succeed, the hunger for power, losses in life, the values we acquire, the indoctrination of religious belief, the experiences of abuse, neglect, and punishment etc. It is believed that the early and positive experiences with the people who first looked after us shape our long-term emotional well-being. When our emotional needs are met or responded to in the first years of life, this has a long-term effect on adulthood, and there is a healthy reciprocal relationship between a child and the caregiver, which is transferred to a relationship with God and others.

The faith development model conceptualizes this psychological process of meaning-making in six stages and suggests that this structure is the same regardless of whether individuals are aligned to a religious or non-religious center of value.

Stages of Faith Development

Pre-Stage—Undifferentiated Faith. Fowler's stages of faith development are divided into six stages that are hierarchal. The first phase which was highly influenced by Erikson's psychosocial development (1950) is regarded as the Pre-Stage with an undifferentiated faith (Moore, 2016, P. 2). According to Fowler (1981), children from birth to about three years of age have the potential for faith but lack the ability to act on that potential. Through loving care from parents and other adults in their lives, young children start to build a lived experience of trust, courage, hope, and love. According to the psychosocial theory, after the warmth and protection of the womb, the child's first emotional task is to learn how to trust the primary caregiver, without whom the infant will not survive. This trust is reliant upon the baby's developing a sense of the world as a good, loving, and safe place (Nicolson, 2010, p. 143; Hook, 2002, 286). Quoting Erikson (1963), Hook (2002) explains that consistency and sameness are important values for a child so that the child can learn to trust and rely on the providers so that the child can trust the self, and so that the child can trust the capacity of his/her organs to cope with urges (p. 287).

However, when this early stage is severely disturbed by a lack of love and support from the significant others, a great variety of psychopathologies would have their origin in the unsuccessful resolution of this early stage of development, especially when the needs of the child are not met, and this may lead to mistrust, insecurity, self-doubt, inability to love and low self-esteem (Hook, 2002, pp. 287-290). According to Fowler (1981), the individual's understanding of herself or himself in relation to others and to centers of shared value and commitment is essential in the development of faith. Thus, at this early stage, children experience faith as a connection between themselves and their caregivers. In this context, faith begins with a disposition to trust, which is mediated through recognizing the eyes and confirming the smiles of the caregiver (p. 121).

Stage 1: Intuitive-Projective Faith. This is the pre-school aged children (between 3-7 years); the cognitive development of children of this age is such that they are unable to think abstractly and are generally unable to see the world from anyone else's perspective. Here, individuals have developed language and are capable of drawing on stories that have been told to them as well as images they have seen to form conceptions of God (Fowler, 1981, p. 148; Andrade,

2014). Faith is not a thought-out set of ideas, but instead a set of impressions that are largely gained from their parents or other significant adults in their lives. In this way, children become involved with the rituals of their religious community by experiencing them and learning from those around them.

Stage 2: Mythic-Literal Faith (between 6–12 years). Children at this age are able to start to work out the difference between verified facts and things that might be more fantasy or speculation. At this age, children's source of religious authority starts to expand past parents and trusted adults to others in their community like teachers, pastors, religious persons, and friends. They thrive on stories, and for them, these stories provide a central way of establishing identity through learning the stories of their own community (Fowler, 1987, p. 61). However, children can become trapped in stories and in their literal, one-dimensional view of symbols because children think in concrete and literal ways. Thus, faith becomes the stories told and the rituals practiced.

Stage 3: Synthetic-Conventional Faith (between 11–18, and where many adults are) Unlike previous stages, adolescents at this stage are able to think abstractly. What were once simple stories and rituals can now be seen as more cohesive narratives about values and morals. With abstract thinking comes the ability to see layers of meaning in the stories, rituals, and symbols of their faith. At this stage, people start to have the ability to see things from someone else's perspective. This means that they can also imagine what others think about them and their faith. People at this stage claim their faith or value as their own; however, the faith that is claimed is still the faith of their family, especially their parent's religiosity. Individuals here are influenced by puberty and adolescents' development of self-images that are formed based on how they think others see them. Fowler (1981) stated that during this stage, "a person has an 'ideology," a more or less consistent clustering of values and beliefs, but he or she has not objectified it for examination and, in a sense, is unaware of having it" (p. 173).

Stage 4: Individuative-Reflective Faith (from around 18 and above) Here individuals adopt new value systems as a result of exposure to different ways of life. These experiences result in their questioning of the faith traditions they previously had. Prior to this stage, the individuals may have had an uncritical acceptance of others' beliefs as the basis of their own beliefs. The adult may also develop interpersonal multi-perspective cognitions and begin to desire a personal relationship with God in which they feel loved in a deep and comprehensive way (Fowler & Dell, 2005). When an adult can no longer tolerate the diversity of views and roles of previous faith experiences, individuals may truly become individuals by detaching from the defining group or parental religiosity, enabling them to decide for themselves what it is they believe.

Stage 5: Paradoxical-Consolidative (Conjunctive) Faith. (This is rare before age 30 – only 7% of Fowler's total sample are at this stage, although another 8% are in transition toward it. (Fowler, 1986, p. 30). This stage is when the struggles and questioning of stage four give way to a more comfortable place. Some answers have been found and the person at this stage is comfortable knowing that all the answers might not be easily found. In this stage, the strong need for individual self-reflection gives way to a sense of the importance of community in faith development. People at this stage are also much more open to other people's faith perspectives. This is not because they are moving away from their faith but because they have a realization that other people's faith might inform and deepen their own. The individual is able to embrace and integrate opposites and polarities in life and has a deeper appreciation for symbols, stories, metaphors, and myths from their own faith tradition and that from others (Fowler & Dell, 2005). Thus, the individual in this stage no longer relies on others for authority on faith values and beliefs but has fully internalized their own faith values.

Stage 6: Universalizing Faith. (This is a very rare stage, represented by only 0.3% of Fowler's sample (1986). Individuals at this stage are willing to "sacrifice the self and to risk the partial justice of the present order for the sake of a more inclusive justice and the realization of love" (p. 200), The difference between individuals in this stage and those in stage five is that those in stage five merely recognize justice without committing themselves to challenge the existing order, in order to ensure it is a reality for all. Fowler provided Martin Luther King Jr., Mother Theresa, and Gandhi as examples of individuals who reached the sixth stage of faith development.

Fowler describes people at this stage as having a special grace that makes them seem more lucid, simpler, and yet somehow more fully human than the rest of us. People at this stage can become important religious teachers because they have the ability to relate to anyone at any stage and from any faith. They are able to relate without condescension but, at the same time, are able to challenge the assumptions that those of other stages might have. People at this stage cherish life but also do not hold on to life too tightly. They put their faith into action, challenging the status quo and working to create justice in the world.

Fowler's faith development model has been widely used in religious education, Christian pastoral care, and other applied settings. For example, Neuman (2011) suggested using Fowler's model to help pediatric nurses and practitioners address the spiritual needs of children and adolescents in their care. Various instruments have been devised to measure faith development, including the faith development interview (FDI), faith styles scales (FSS), and faith development scale (FDS) (Parker, 2006).

The theory of faith development is significant in this context, particularly the pre-stage-undifferentiated faith. It explores how consistent love and care from parents and other adults in a child's life can assist the child in developing a lived experience of trust, courage, hope, and love. In simpler terms, a child's ability to trust depends on their capacity to perceive the world as a good, loving, and safe place.

The theory is also important because it focuses on the psychosocial development of an individual and respects and/or protects a person's meaning-making capacity. It takes seriously the narrative structure of the life history of religious women and men. This is because life history is important to faith and religious development. Actually, the entire project of faith development theory consists of telling developmental stories, and recognizing how these stories impact the life of the individual (Streib 2005, p. 111). In telling and retelling their faith developmental stories, men and women religious will learn the efficacious way of coping with crises and dealing with stress in order to attain psychological well-being.

It helps individuals reflect on their faith journey and how they have grown. Faith development instruments, especially the faith development interview (FDI), faith styles scales (FSS), and faith development scale (FDS), can be applied to determine how a person's faith has grown or the crises of faith among religious men and women, their struggles in cultivating spirituality, or abandoning religious life.

It is also important for men and women religious because it serves as a new conversation between religion and psychology, directing fresh attention to the relationship between the structures of personality and the contents of religious faith.

One of the benefits of Fowler's model is its coverage over the whole lifespan which exceeds previous development models which only focused on childhood and adolescence (Coyle, 2011).

Additionally, the broad definition of "faith" enables the model to be applied to a wide range of religious and non-religious domains.

Understanding faith development theory is crucial for this work because the development of faith in early childhood is a complex process that requires a supportive and trusting environment to be navigated effectively. This suggests that individuals who develop an appropriate foundation of trust and faith during childhood are more likely to experience stable religious development and find meaning in life, even when faced with life challenges as adults.

Religious Faith Development and Childhood Experiences

How did your faith in God develop as an individual? Who introduced you to faith and how was it done? What was your first image of God? Did you perceive God as a judge, an all-seeing eye looking down on your mistakes and recording them in His eternal book? Or did you envision a figure with an overgrown or huge white beard, holding a big stick and recording your good and bad behavior? Did your parents ever tell you to obey God, warning that failure to do so would result in eternal condemnation to hellfire?

Children learn by observing other people and patterning their behavior after theirs. As children copy the behavior of their parents, so also they adapt to the religion of their parents without question. As children mature, they are oriented to the religion of their family, their beliefs, and practices. Although the child might be copying the behavior of the parents, this might be mostly extrinsic or immature religiosity, as described by Allport and Ross (1967). Extrinsic religious orientation is a method of using religion to achieve non-religious goals, essentially viewing religion as a means to an end (Batson, 1982). It is used by people who go to religious gatherings and claim certain religious ideologies to establish or maintain social networks while minimally adhering to the teachings of the religion.

Religious faith develops and matures in a child through experiences of God. A child may have knowledge about the "god" introduced by parents or taught in school; however, the child may not have a personal relationship or faith in this "god." Faith in God develops when one owns this faith, which begins with personal experience or encounter with God.

The development of religious faith in children and adolescents is an area of increasing interest to developmental psychologists. In their research, Bellamy, Mou, and Castle (2004) explain that parents have a significant influence of 55% on the religious development of their children. Mothers were a significant influence in the religious development of about 50%, while fathers were influential for a lesser number of 33% (p. 4).

Some of the participants had wonderful parents who introduced them to God, and that experience helped them develop a loving relationship with Him. Below are their stories:

"I was baptized when I was born, and since then, my faith has continued to grow as I watch my parents live out their faith. We used to say the rosary before meals, which made me salivate and hate praying the rosary because it is too long as we waited forever for food. However, after my personal experience with God, I entered into a deeper relationship with Him, and I love Mother Mary. Praying the rosary is now a blessing and extend this blessing to my community members."

"When I was a child, I pictured God as a father figure with a large white beard. I was initially fearful of God. I enjoyed attending church with them and serving at the altar to avoid punishment from God. Despite losing my parents to war, I held onto the faith they had instilled in me. After having a personal encounter with God, my perception of Him has been transformed."

"As a family, we prayed together before meals, before bedtime, and after waking up. We prayed the rosary daily. This helped me develop a devotion to Mary. However, my initial perception of God was of a punishing God, always watching and keeping track of my sins. As I matured in my faith, I encountered a loving God rather than a punishing God."

"The church was close to our house, and we attended Mass daily as a family. When I was a young adult, I belonged to the choir and regularly participated in the activities of our Small Christian Community. My parents' strong religious values had a big impact on me. They used to tell me to obey God, warning me that if I didn't, God would punish me. I grew up with both a deep love for and fear of God."

"My parents were poor but dedicated to church activities, and my faith developed from them. However, my perception of God was that of a judging God who would condemn me to hell if I made a mistake and I feared Him. As I mature in my faith, my relationship with God grows and my trust in Him becomes stronger."

"As a family, we prayed together and attended Small Christian Community events, which my father chaired for many years. This influenced my faith, and my love for God developed from my personal encounter with Him."

"My parents were incredibly devoted and loving. As a child, I saw my father as having a character similar to God's. I love God just as my parents taught me."

The love that children receive from their parents often shapes their perception of God. Those who had loving parents often reflect that love in their relationship with God, although others may fear

God due to negative perceptions instilled in them during childhood. On the other hand, people who have had difficult experiences in childhood may have a distorted view of God due to their emotional wounds. In his study, Bierman (2005) examined and discovered that,

> Paternal abuse has a significant negative effect on religious involvement, belief, and religious self-concept in children. The most obvious explanation for this pattern of results involves the identification of God as a paternal figure. Individuals who are brought up with harsh, capricious fathers form a negative view of paternal figures. This negative view of paternal figures that victims of paternal abuse may form from their experiences could lead them to distance themselves from these celestial paternal figures, leading to a decrease in religious activities and self-perceived religiosity. (p. 357)

This is true because when a child faces abuse, neglect, or an attitude of hatred from the parents, the child automatically feels unloved and insecure. This lack of love from parents is also translated and interpreted by the child as a lack of love from God, whom the parents introduced the child to. The child may feel that God also does not love him/her. That is why some people prefer to call God "Mother" rather than "Father."

As narrated above, this was Fr. James's experience. His image of God was much crueler and more sadistic than ordinary earthly fathers. He felt rejected by God just as he felt imaginary rejection from his parents, brothers, and sisters. Two participants explained how their lives became very empty and depressing after sexual abuse. This trauma affected their trust in God as a father figure. From all these narrations, one can deduce that faith in God can be wounded or marred by childhood negative experiences. Thus, faith requires a trusting and supportive environment to be negotiated meaningfully (Fowler, 1981, p. 18). When an individual's value or faith is marred, the person may easily despair in life, feel insecure, or hate God, which may lead to frustration and, consequently, immature coping strategies.

When healthy interactions do not take place or if the significant other's care is unreliable, it may lead to mental, behavioral, and emotional impairment. If childhood negative experiences could affect the brain as explained above, subsequently, it could also affect an adult's faith or religious development. Some of the traumatic experiences that can mar the religious development of a child include: neglect and/or extreme poverty, a violent household, sexual or verbal abuse, separation or divorce of parents, losing a parent or sibling, a mentally ill or addicted parent, experiencing a natural disaster, terrorist attack, or war. The aftermath of these experiences in an adult's life may include: immature coping skills, relationship imbalance, bullying, incessant anger, low self-image and self-concept, lack of trust, and insecure attachment.

Religious men and women are not immune or exempted from this early upbringing and its negative and/or positive consequences on their religious faith. This implies that negative childhood experiences of men and women may lead to interpersonal and/or intrapersonal difficulties in adulthood, thus leading to despair, frustration, and maybe psychological problems.

Consequences of Wounded Faith among Religious Persons

Experiences show that when neglect or abuse of any kind is a reality in a child's life, the person who survived this scenario often feels ashamed to talk about their childhood adversity for fear of being asked to leave religious life. This makes it difficult to recognize that these events occur among religious persons. While it is easier to turn away than to face these issues, we can no longer hide the stress, mental challenges, depression, substance abuse, anxiety disorder, insecure attachment/behavior, and all the trauma-related issues that plague religious institutes today.

> Cyrus Ombati, reporting on Tuesday, February 1st, 2011, for *The Standard Newspaper*, Kenya, recounted how a Catholic nun burned herself to death using petrol after receiving a letter from their headquarters in Nairobi informing her that she had been dismissed from the order.
>
> On May 22nd, 2018, *Lesotho Times* carried news of a 35-year-old Roman Catholic priest who allegedly gunned down a 35-year-old nun, Pascalinah Kabi. The shocking incident occurred at Maryland Mission in Leribe District during the early hours of Friday, May 18th, 2018, with close sources saying this could have been a crime of passion as the two were in a relationship. The suspect handed himself over to the police, *Lesotho Times* concluded.
>
> On July 28, 2018, ABC News (USA) recounted the story of some Sisters from Chile who took a trip to the Vatican City for the #MeToo Movement in protest of the sexual

abuse by priests. According to the story, a sister wearing a full religious habit and clutching her rosary, broke nearly two decades of silence to tell AP about the moment in the year 2000 when the priest to whom she was confessing her sins forced himself on her during the sacrament of confession. The assault — and a subsequent advance by a different priest a year later — led her to stop going to confession with any priest other than her spiritual father, who lives in a different country.

On Wednesday, 19th September 2018, Kenya *Daily Nation* carried a story of a Catholic priest in Trans Nzoia County in Kenya who was charged with attempting to defile a minor. (*Daily Nation*, Wednesday, Sept. 19, 2018, pg. 3).

Two religious women, during the interview, confessed how they were victims of sexual exploitation at the hands of some priests when they were seeking help. On Tuesday, February 5th, 2019, Pope Francis acknowledged that the Roman Catholic Church had faced a persistent problem of sexual abuse of nuns by priests and even bishops. He commented on this during a news conference aboard the papal plane returning to Rome from his trip to the United Arab Emirates. Pope Francis expressed that it was a continuing problem and that the Vatican was working on it (Horowitz & Dias, 2019, P. A1).

On June 28th, 2009, Alex Kiprotich, reporting for *The Standard Newspaper,* explained that society has put high expectations on nuns and priests, which has affected them. Echoing the words of a nun, Kiprotich explained that this high expectation of them has made some become so ashamed of their shortcomings in indecent acts that some resort to suicide rather than face society, especially if they are expelled from the convent.

What could have happened in the lives of these individuals that moved them toward deviant behavior? How stable was their faith and/or basic trust in themselves as they grew and matured into adulthood?

These questions are difficult to answer, but the information gathered from the experiences of those interviewed in this work sheds light on some reasons behind the crises many religious people face in living a vowed life. The theories of Erikson and Fowler guided this work by discovering how the consistency of love and support, or lack of them, from parents or significant others, impacted the faith life of some men and women religious interviewed in this work. Consistency of love and care are important values for a child to learn to trust themselves and their providers. In trusting self, the child grows up with the capacity to trust others, God, and the environment and cope with life challenges. The initial trust children develop serves as a connection to their caregivers and is crucial for the later development of faith in adulthood.

This chapter introduces Fowler's theory of faith development, which explains how an individual's faith evolves and matures. It also discusses the relevance of this theory to the current work and examines how parents' religious beliefs influence the religious development of their children. The following chapter will analyze the experiences of several religious men and women who were interviewed during the course of this work.

CHAPTER FOUR

Influence of Childhood Experiences on Faith Development

"Religious Orders are not formed for the purpose of gathering together perfect people but those who have the courage to aim at perfection."

—St. Francis de Sales

In this chapter, we share the stories collected from religious individuals who were interviewed and consented for their stories to be included in the book. The data was analyzed based on the questions asked of the participants and categorized into three sections corresponding to the subheadings of each question. The writer refrained from using names during the transcription.

SECTION 1: Childhood Experiences of Participants

Question: How would you describe your childhood experiences prior to 12 years?

This question aims to understand the participants' childhood experiences. They were asked to choose from three options: "caring," "neglected," or "I am not sure." Each option was accompanied by an explanation of what it meant for the participant.

Below are some of the responses of some religious persons who experienced care and love:

"My mother was always there for me and took great care of me. Similarly, I am always there for those who are suffering in my parish. I am very generous, and sometimes people take advantage of my kind heart. However, I missed the love of my father."

"Although my father was strict and wanted orderliness in our home, he is very compassionate and loving to all his children. My mother was very cool and loving. I learned to be assertive and disciplined through my father. I don't give up easily and I am a happy religious.

My mother was very strict and left my father when I was very young, but my father was very caring. I was so close to my father, and I always ate with him. He spoilt me with love. He taught me how to love and how to work hard and not despair when life is tough. However, I missed my mother's love."

"My dad was strict; however, he disciplined us with love and care. I always consider myself lucky when it comes to parental care. I felt secure in their arms. I relate to people around me in the same way. I am firm, assertive, but kind."

"I am the first son, so all the attention and love was on me. I was lavished with love. I also have a good sense of humor. My community members enjoy and love being around me. I use my gift always to give them life. Although I experienced violence at school, I was loved by my parents. My mother was very kind and compassionate. When I was bullied in school by a teacher, this experience put me down and I developed a phobia for school. I was no longer performing well academically. But when I got into another school, my self-confidence returned and I was very good in class again. This transformation was possible because of the change, and because the trust in self was instilled in me when I was young. My father entrusted some hard tasks to me and I was very creative as a child to carry them out."

"My parents were just wonderful! I would like to have them again as my parents. They taught me how to love and to be loved. I can say that this caring attitude of my parents instilled a good self-confidence in me."

"My parents were very loving and very humble. I learned much from their simplicity and humility. I love them. And this gave me a good self-image and self-confidence that I can stand anywhere and talk about life. I am a happy religious."

"My mother was very loving. Despite our poverty, she worked extra hard to ensure that we received a good education and had our basic needs met. Her dedication and hard work served as a model for me. As a result, I developed a strong sense of creativity and optimism. While others may see darkness, I always see light and a way out, particularly in challenging situations."

"I was loved so much that I wasn't allowed to do any house chores. I share the same love with those around me. People tend to gather around me, and I teach them how to think positively. However, I must admit that I struggle with laziness and procrastination."

"My parents were very kind and loving. Our home was always filled with relatives because Dad was very welcoming and hospitable. They modeled hospitality for me and I love helping people."

"My parents were very caring, especially my Mum. My father died early but my mother became the breadwinner of the family. His death was devastating, but my siblings and I were consoled by our kind mother. The love that my father showed me, and all his instructions before his death stayed with me and helped me with life's challenges."

"I was the first son and the only son among many girls so I was cared for by my mother. My mother was very loving. Father was mostly away and returned at night with many good things for me. I missed those good old days. This love is reflected in the way I relate with those around me. I extend the same love to people around me, and they feel comfortable with me."

Analysis

All of these religious men and women have one thing in common: they have pleasant personalities and are easy to talk to. They seem to be happy and are very open to answering all the questions posed to them. This shows a sign of trust and security, which a child develops in a caring environment. Lewis-Morrarty, Degnan, Chronis-Tuscano, Pine, Henderson, & Fox (2015) concurred with this when they observed 165 babies and concluded that the experiences of constant love and care from parents may develop in a child and subsequently in an adult, a sense of trust and security.

Most of them were very punctual for the interview and responded to the questions with calmness. Those who were a few minutes late called ahead of time to let me know they would be late.

They seemed to have good self-image and self-confidence, which was shown in their gentle and confident responses to my questions.

They seemed to be happy in their lives as religious people, and most of them confessed that they were very happy in the life they had chosen. Some of them came from a staunch and devoted Christian family background and were influenced by the religious devotion of their caregivers.

This is in line with the theories of Erikson and Fowler that consistent love and support develop in a child a sense of security, love, and trust. Erikson echoed: If the care the infant receives is consistent, predictable, and reliable, they will develop a sense of trust which they will carry with them to other relationships, and they will be able to feel secure even when threatened (McLeod, 2013). Fowler (1981) concurred that at this early stage, children experience faith as a connection between themselves and their caregivers. In this context, faith begins with a disposition to trust, which is mediated through recognizing the eyes and confirming the smiles of the caregiver (p. 121).

"I Am Not Sure" Responses:

"My parents were very loving when I was a child. We lived peacefully and happily. However, the death of my twin brothers affected my parents' relationship. My father became very aggressive and a bully, while my mother was living in fear of him and helplessness. This condition affected me, and my reaction was to live in fear too, to withdraw emotionally from people around me, and I live with bitterness till today."

This is consistent with the research carried out among children who witnessed violence that emotional and physical abuse were found to be associated with thought patterns characterized by themes of mistrust, abandonment, defectiveness, domineering, or avoidance disorder (Messman-Moore & Coates, 2007).

"My parents were loving, but they corrected my mistake with severity. I was expected to be number one in everything and not to make mistakes. I ended up making many mistakes for fear of my father's voice. Today, I have made so many mistakes in my life that I no longer care. I was arrogant and rebellious, and I did the opposite of what my father would want me to do, just to make him feel bad."

"My father was always absent for business. My mum was available but strict. Because I loved my father more than my mum, I developed an insecure attachment toward him. I was jealous of my mother, and I used to share a bed with my father. But my mother would take me to my bed when I fell asleep. I hated my mum so much for "stealing" my father's love from me. I used to disobey and disrespect my mother, especially when my dad was around."

From the experiences of those who chose the "I am not sure" option to describe their childhood experiences, it is clear that they lacked the consistent love of one of their parents at the initial stages of psychosocial development, where trust is built in a child. One was fixated on Freud's phallic stage, where boys are jealous of their fathers and girls are jealous of their mothers (Electra complex). Another got fixated at the anal stage, where the strictness of parents can communicate a lack of love to the child. According to Freud, children who experience problems at this stage may become adults who are mean, stubborn, rigid, obsessively orderly, etc., because of the strictness of their parents.

Experiences of Neglect Responses:

"My mother left our house when I was two years old because my father was very abusive and was having a relationship with another woman. My father brought a nanny to care for me but my nanny was wicked too. She could hit and slap me and warned me not to tell my father. I grew up with the feeling of insecurity, rejection, and low self-image."

"My parents were full-time employed government workers, so they provided my two siblings and me with a nanny. Mary, our nanny, loved my siblings much but disliked me. She used to starve me and hit me with a cane when I made a mistake. Most of the time, she punished me by starving me and threatening not to give me food for a whole day if I exposed her behavior. So, I grew up with much fear and anxiety."

"My father was an alcohol addict. He abused my mother physically and emotionally. He used all his money on drinking and sometimes he would sleep along the road where he had fallen. This brought a lot of shame to the family. Mother was so helpless and we only cried with her. This affected me so much that I vowed never to touch alcohol. However, I could be violent, very bitter, aggressive, and use rude words to my community members."

"My father was a drunkard. He came home almost every night drunk and rained abuses on my poor mother. As a child, I watched him with helplessness and powerlessness because I couldn't defend my mother. My only consolation was to cry with my mother. Today I drink a lot. I had vowed never to touch alcohol, but it is difficult to come clean."

A few participants experienced abandonment from their mothers, and this experience made them seek attention from a mother figure. A few participants were sexually abused when they were very young. This experience left them with guilt, shame, self-blame, and insecurity. Some participants were victims of war and genocide, and the trauma of watching relatives killed and raped still affected them. A few of the respondents suffered neglect because of the divorce of their parents. Additionally, some participants experienced the loss of one or both parents, leading to the children being left in the care of relatives who mistreated them.

Analysis

From the stories of those who had adverse childhood experiences, it is obvious that some are living bitter lives. Those who were wounded through sexual abuse lacked self-esteem and exhibited a lot of fear, shame, self-blame, and insecurity. Most of them wailed so much during the interview session that it felt like the interview was becoming a counseling session. After the interview, some participants were provided with therapy sessions, while many were referred to where they could get help.

Some religious persons did not show up for their scheduled interviews, while others called to cancel. Many arrived late, and several were unwilling to meet in person, so we conducted the interviews over the phone.

Almost all the participants who experienced unhappy childhood passage, apart from those who are currently undergoing therapy sessions, confess a lack of self-confidence, low self-esteem, and bitterness. Some have resorted to coping with alcohol and are seriously addicted to alcohol and social media. The experience indicates that their initial trust in their significant other was shattered and may potentially impact them in adulthood. Freud, Fowler and Erickson opined that the initial trust a child develops is very vital because it is a connection between themselves and their caregiver and the hallmark for subsequent personality development in adult life. This is consistent with the research carried out by Loken and Reigstad (2012), as explained above, that children who have been physically abused or neglected often have insecure attachment and suffer long-term consequences in adulthood, such as trust issues, anger-related issues, relationship imbalance, low self-esteem, inappropriate coping skills, a feeling of powerlessness, internalization of aggression, depression, and anxiety (p. 39).

Those who experienced rejection confessed that sometimes they feel very insecure and believe that they will also be rejected in religious life. So, they live in fear and do not enjoy religious life. Some wish to be out of religious life, but they do not know how to face the rejection of the people and the "imaginary" shame that goes with leaving religious life.

This is in line with Freud's theory that the unconscious mind governs an adult's behavior to a greater degree, and when a child is traumatized, punished, threatened, abused, neglected, treated with contempt, and separated from parents due to death or divorce, the child gets fixated, and the consequences may include: fear, insecurity, compulsive obsessive behaviors, low self-image, lack of trust, etc., (Ellis et al., 112). Similarly, Erikson opined that when the care of the significant other is missing, harsh or inconsistent, unpredictable, and unreliable, then the infant will develop a sense of mistrust and will not have confidence in the world around them or in their abilities to influence events (McLeod, 2013).

This finding implies that many consecrated persons who are raised in loving families grow into high-functioning adults with good self-confidence and self-worth, and they have more constructive coping strategies in difficult times than those who experience neglect or abuse.

Question: Were you exposed to violence or abuse when you were growing up?

In answering this question, two options of "Yes" and "No" were given, after which the participants were given the opportunity to explain their choice.

Responses to the "Yes" option are explained below:

A few participants experienced physical, sexual, or emotional violence from their fathers. Some yell like their fathers in the community. Some bully, insult, and behave arrogantly, which affects their community members.

According to one participant: "I experienced physical abuse from her father, and thus, I developed incessant anger. I get irritated over small issues, and my community members fear me. I was not aware of their fear until one of them confronted me with courage. Sometimes I feel so depressed and wonder why I don't have a steady relationship and why I am isolated."

A few participants watched as their fathers physically assaulted their mothers, and it is affecting them as adults because they are somewhat violent and aggressive. Very few were sexually abused, and they expressed that they are always moody in the community; they feel insecure, lonely, incessantly angry, and always clean themselves. They used withdrawal as a coping skill, afraid of men and blaming themselves for what had happened.

A participant places too many unrealistic expectations on herself and others because her father's voice kept telling her, "You have to be number one." Some participants experienced the emotional torture of war. According to one respondent: "Most nights, I have nightmares because of the ugly experience of war. I get angry easily, and I use passive aggression when I am hurt."

Some were abandoned by their mothers due to separation. A few experienced the death of their mother when they were born: "Growing up without a mother led to years of depression for me." According to Freud, these are fixated at the oral stage, where the breast of the mother feeds and comforts a child, and the mother's smile depicts love. As explained above, the experience of the absence of a mother can lead to fixation at stage one, which may end up developing in adult violent behavior or the problem of eating, drinking, smoking, addiction of every kind, or immature personality. Some participants experienced the death of one parent, which led to their being cared for by extended relatives.

Analysis

The careful analysis of the respondents' views reveals the devastating effects of the experiences of emotional and physical violence on some religious men and women. According to Ogbuji (2015), when a child watches his or her father abusing and physically assaulting the mother, that child may be inclined to practice the same behavior in the future, especially when the said child does not go through a healing process. This hostile behavior, apparently, will eventually turn into bullying, antagonistic, brutal, destructive, and vicious lifestyle, especially when that child is not helped (p. 51). This is in line with the literature used in this work, such as Vandervender (2014), Bruwer, et al. (2013), Messman-Moore and Coates (2007), Busby, Walker, and Holman (2011) that childhood maltreatment can influence adult relationships, such that individuals with a history of physical abuse report more conflict and more negative evaluations of self and others.

The theories of Erikson and Fowler also echoed the same findings that negative childhood experiences affect an adult's development and may likely lead to fixations, immature coping skills, relationship imbalance, bullying, incessant anger, low self-image and self-concept, lack of trust, and insecure attachment. Thus, the absence of consistent love, neglect, abuse, violence, unkind words, etc., may lead to mistrust, shame, guilt, an inferiority complex, role confusion, isolation, and despair (Scheck, 2005, p. 4).

SECTION 2: Childhood Experiences of Parental Religious Practices

This section investigates the childhood experiences of parental religious practices that impacted the faith development of some participants.

Question: How would you describe your childhood Religious/faith development?

The participants were given two options, positive and challenging, and then each gave reasons for the option they chose.

The religious persons who had positive faith development are mostly those who received care and love from their parents; the remaining participants are those who may have had challenging childhood experiences, but their parents were faithful Christians. Some of their stories are below:

"From childhood, I have always experienced the love of God through my parents. I love God, and I love the people around me, even those who are difficult to love. I tried to do to others what I would love done to me (the golden rule). My parents taught me that rule from childhood, and I have lived it out in my life. I am a very happy religious."

"I love God, and I know he loves me first. I enjoy every moment with Him, even when life is blurring. I can say I am in a deeper relationship with God. My parents taught me the love of God through their love for me. I love religious life, and I feel privileged and happy that God called me to serve him. I love my ministry, too. My role as a leader in the congregation is life-giving."

"My God is great! He is also good even when things are not rosy. I trust him totally because my mother taught me how to trust. I am confident that he will not put me to shame. When things are tough, I just laugh and say, 'This too shall pass.'"

"God is so good to me. I love God, and I have a deeper relationship with God. I also extend this relationship to my community members. We relate like loving brothers. When some members come with their struggles to put tension in the community, my humor dissipates the tense environment and calms everyone down. They tell me that I have a pleasant personality. That attitude I inherited from my mother."

"My parents were strict and unintentionally introduced me to a punishing God. However, I love God and serve Him and the people around me with joy. I am a happy religious person, and my happiness is a gift to the community, although my unconscious strictness gets in the way sometimes."

Many participants echoed that they are in a deeper relationship with God, and even when religious life is not rosy, their faith in God is not shaken, but previously, their image of God was judging and punishing God. These results support the established knowledge that a parent who is committed to regular attendance of church services, charitable activities, and active participation in the church's activities can have a positive impact on their children's development (Schultz & Schultz, 2009; Bellamy, Mou, & Castle, 2004; Bierman, 2005; Regnerus & Elder, 2003; Kabiru, 2014, Gyimah, 2013). Most of the interviewees who were brought up in a caring and religious environment ended up developing religious faith through participating in the religious activities of their significant others and personal experience of God. It is also consistent with Fowler's theory (1981), that children from birth to about three years of age have the potential for faith but lack the ability to act on that potential. However, through loving care from parents and other adults in their lives, young children start to build a lived experience of trust, courage, hope, and love as they encounter God in a personal way.

Parents, especially mothers, played an important role in modelling faith in God in children. 47.5% of the religious men and women interviewed in this work were cared for by their mothers and were also introduced to the faith by their mothers. They were impacted by their mothers' prayerful nature, caring life, and love, even when their fathers might be uncaring. This is consistent with the research carried out by Bellamy, Mou, and Castle (2004), as explained above: mothers have a significant influence on the religious development of their children, about 50%, while fathers are influential for a lesser number, 33% (p. 4). The remaining 52.5% of those interviewed were initiated to faith in God by either the parent, the father alone, grandparents, siblings, relatives, missionaries/religious, Catholic schools, and parish priests.

It goes without saying that parental religiosity, belief, and spirituality have a more powerful impact on a child's religious development. The more religious the parents are, the more likely their children are to attend religious meetings later in life. This is because children see their parents as role models. The level of religiosity in the parents can also influence their children's religious development through direct and indirect influences, such as parenting behavior, charitable acts, forgiveness, consistent prayer life, an optimistic attitude toward life, etc.

Challenging Faith Development

Those who faced challenges during the early development of their religious faith are mostly those who experienced wars, genocide, rape, physical and emotional abuse, lack of love, neglect, isolation, rejection, as well as the death of a parent. Most of them came to the experience of faith or encounter with God during their adolescent or adult stage of life, either through the high school they attended, or through parish activities or through friends, missionaries, and their parish priests. A few of their stories are narrated below:

"I came to faith through the nuns who taught us in high school. My grandmother forbade me from attending church services with other children because she was pagan."

"My parents were not Christians; I came to faith through the parish priest in my village who was a missionary.

Some participants also confessed how the missionaries in their area inspired faith in them. According to one: "When I lost my parents, my aunt took care of me. But she was not too religious, so I came to the experience of faith through the missionaries in my parish and my parish priest." Another said: "I lived with my grandparents because my mother left our family when my father's relatives made life unbearable for her. My grandmother was not a Christian. So, I encountered God and became a Christian when I joined high school."

Those with negative childhood experiences showed lower levels of faith-related issues until adulthood, which is in line with the research carried out by Regnerus & Elder (2003) that badly treated children report lower levels of importance of faith than well-treated children.

For example, individuals who have experienced war, the death of loved ones, rape, parental abuse, rejection, or extreme poverty in their families often viewed God as cruel and unkind during their childhood. However, their personal encounters with God as adults transformed their attitudes and perceptions of God. One expressed: "I often wonder why a compassionate God took my father at such a young age."

A small number of the respondents were angry with God because of their childhood experiences. One respondent confessed: "I was angry with God because of the kind of 'father' God gave me. I thought God was wicked after my sexual abuse. I could not accept God as a father figure for many years. The feelings of rejection and self-blame clouded my trust in God and others. However, through therapy and the grace of healing from God, my relationship with God has been transformed and renewed."

A few people illustrated how violence shaped their view of God because their father was physically abusing their mother. They wished that God was not a father figure. All responses from this work point to the fact that many factors influence religious development, and the most important are environmental factors, parental influence, community influence, school influence, peer group influence, etc. When childhood experience is adversely affected, it shapes the faith and trust a child has in the significant other, which unconsciously may color adult relationships with self, others, and God.

Obviously, "when mother cow is chewing grass, its young ones watched its mouth," says Chinua Achebe (Things Fall Apart, 1959). Billy Graham puts it well that "The greatest legacy one can pass on to one's children and grandchildren is not money or other material things accumulated in one's life, but rather a legacy of character and faith." This means that children learn by what they see their parents do, and not necessarily by what they hear them say. Another African proverb states that "the child of the crab walks sideways like its mother." An old parable explained it well:

> One day, Mother Crab and her daughter came out from their home to take a walk on the sand. "Child," said the mother, "you are walking very ungracefully. You should accustom yourself to walking straightforwardly. Why, in the world, do you walk sideways like that?" "Mother," said the young one, "set the example yourself, and I will follow you. For I walk exactly as I see you walk."

When parents do not set good examples for their children, especially in learning to love and be loved, in learning to trust and be trusted, in learning to forgive and be forgiven, in learning to give as they have received, it affects their future relationships with themselves, others, and God. That is why some adults feel as if God does not love them. They experience insecurity, a low self-image, and a lack of self-love, and they feel incapable of doing what they could ordinarily do. All the evidence above points to the fact that parental religiosity has an enormous impact on adults' religiosity. The children who experienced consistent love from their significant others are positively impacted. On the other hand, religious persons who are affected negatively question their faith in God. Some of them are unhappy and wish to leave religious life, but they still have the desire to serve God. Their coping mechanism is waiting on God.

SECTION 3: Psychotherapy Intervention Strategies

This section explores therapy intervention strategies that can promote the comprehensive healing of the participants.

Question: Which caregiver would you approach for help on issues connected to childhood experiences and why?

The majority of the participants prefer to approach a therapist, a good number of those interviewed prefer to meet a spiritual director, and very few participants prefer to talk to a friend.

Those who prefer a therapist:

Many believe that therapy can help them explore feelings of anger, low self-image, insecurity, addiction to alcohol, and their relationships with others. Some need therapy to address self-blame resulting from experiences of incest and sexual abuse, and to rebuild self-confidence. Others seek therapy to work through feelings of rejection, negative attitudes toward their mother/father, depression, and bitterness. Some individuals require help in forgiving their parents and overcoming the urge to bully others as a coping mechanism. One expressed: "I need counseling sessions to help me gather the courage to forgive my father. I understand that forgiveness is also a form of grace. I also need to gain self-confidence and empowerment to make a decision about my religious life because I am not happy. I want to be able to have my own family." Another echoed: "I need a therapist to help me deal with my loneliness in the midst of my community members, my low self-concept, and my addictions to social media. To dispose myself to be loved rather than living a lonely life and to be empowered to make a decision about this life."

Some seek help to forgive their father and learn to manage their anger and arrogance. Others are already in therapy seeking help to deal with fear and become more comfortable with who they are. Some interviewees who are dealing with the grief of war and the loss of a loved one also echoed the same need. One said: "I fear death since my father's death. I need a therapist to help me deal with the phobia of death and accept its reality." Another said: "The experience of war was traumatic and my dreams were filled with this horror and nightmares. I am getting help." An interviewee revealed: "I still remember with reminiscence how my relatives were butchered like animals. Sometimes I tried to deny it, but it was real. I need help from a counselor to be healed from the trauma of war."

Those who prefer a Spiritual Director:

Those who choose a spiritual director and have spiritual directors seek spiritual growth, a better relationship with God and others, improvement in their prayer life, and a healthy religious life. Many religious individuals in this group have undergone therapy and feel empowered. They're looking for a spiritual director to help them strengthen their faith and relationships with God and others, deal with times when prayer feels dry, and face daily religious challenges by becoming more reflective, accepting imperfection, and being gentle with themselves and others.

Those who prefer a friend:

These religious individuals prefer sharing with a friend because they believe that a friend would understand them better. They claim to be afraid of being vulnerable before another person but could confide in friends who understand them.

Summary

At the conclusion of the interview, most participants recognized the necessity for therapy and suggested that it should be considered essential in religious institutions. These religious persons believed that therapy would help them deal with the issues of managing their anger, empower them to gain self-confidence, help them deal with their insecure attachment, negative attitude toward life and self, bullying and violent behavior, insecurity, bitterness, addiction to alcohol and social media.

It is important for wounded individuals to go through a therapeutic process to attain the stage of Paradoxical-Consolidative Faith (Fowler and Dell, 2005). According to Fowler, individuals who reach the fifth stage in faith development can embrace opposites and challenges in life and have a deeper appreciation for life. They no longer rely on others for authority on faith, values, and beliefs but have fully internalized their faith values. Therapeutic processes or spiritual directions will help in attaining this stage and becoming comfortable in enjoying life, knowing that all the answers to faith and God might not be easily found. However, their strong faith and relationship with God and others may give way to the importance of living joyfully their lives as religious persons.

Most of the issues that adult religious persons are dealing with, which are hindering them from attaining the fifth stage of faith development, emanate from childhood negative and traumatic experiences, which unfortunately continue through adult life. According to Draucker & Martsolf (2006), counseling intervention is a need for an individual who is wounded by negative experiences during childhood (P. 2). When the process of healing is in progress, the individual may likely reach stage six in faith development. This stage, Fowler explained, is a very rare stage to reach because individuals at this stage are willing to "sacrifice the self and to risk the partial justice of the present order for the sake of a more inclusive justice and the realization of love" (Fowler, 1981, p. 200).

Stage six could be the desire of every religious person because individuals at stage six have special grace that makes them seem more lucid, simpler, and yet somehow more fully human. They cherish life but also do not hold on to life too tightly. They put their faith into action, challenging the status quo and working to create justice in the world. To live a more fulfilling and happy life as a religious person is the goal of every consecrated person. This may not be realized when one is unconsciously battling and dragging along with the wounds one sustained through negative life experiences.

Question: Are there other issues you would like to talk about?

In response to this question, participants were allowed to raise any other issues they wanted to discuss. Many of them emphasized the importance of providing therapeutic assistance to candidates seeking to join religious life, as it is essential for their interpersonal relationships within communities. "I will suggest that each congregation makes counseling sessions available to religious at the initial and ongoing stages of formation because we all need healing, and we are wounded. A healed religious person will become an effective religious." Formation in religious life needs to be holistic. Many religious individuals have experienced emotional wounds from a young age, and their current actions may stem from these past experiences. It's important to address these issues. We understand that religious life is meant for imperfect individuals who require assistance in their personal growth. It's undeniable that therapy and spiritual guidance can be effective paths for emotional healing.

Conclusion

This work demonstrates that consecrated individuals are not immune to the negative effects of childhood trauma. These unhappy childhood experiences can have long-lasting effects on adults if the individuals do not seek proper help. Problems such as behavioral issues, lack of self-regulation, inability to control one's appetite, emotional and psychological health issues, poor planning and prioritizing abilities, procrastination, lack of resilience, issues with social skills and relationships, inability to focus, depression, irrational behavior, low self-esteem, anxiety disorders, poor coping skills, and self-doubt can be linked to negative childhood experiences. Therapy sessions and the healing grace of God can help individuals manage stress and deal with childhood trauma and its effects on adult life. This can lead to better relationships, improved behavioral issues, and better coping mechanisms for life's challenges.

It's important to note that not everyone who experiences childhood trauma will be affected as adults. This means that two children from the same family who experience the same trauma may respond differently, with one being resilient and the other experiencing symptoms throughout their life. Seeking help and embarking on the journey toward healing and wholeness is, therefore, crucial to living a healthy and joyful life. The next chapter will explore different therapies used in helping wounded individuals.

CHAPTER FIVE

Understanding Psychotherapy Process

"The secret of change is to focus all your energy, not on fighting the old, but on building the new."

— Socrates

A person who is wounded through childhood adverse experiences needs to go through a healing process to facilitate behavior change. Psychology, the scientific study of the mind and behavior, utilizes psychotherapy or therapy in its treatment process. Psychotherapy is a compound Greek word: *psychē,* which means soul, and *therapeuō,* which means heal or cure. (Brownell, 2010, p.4). Literally, it means the process that heals the soul by making the client healthy and sound of mind.

Psychotherapy, as a helping process, aims at improving an individual's well-being and mental health, alleviating troublesome behaviors, beliefs, compulsions, thoughts, or emotions, and improving relationships and social skills. Psychological therapy, according to Feltham & Dryden (2004), is a principled relationship characterized by the application of one or more psychological theories and a recognized set of communication skills, modified by experience, intuition, and other interpersonal factors, to a client's intimate concerns, problems or aspirations. Its predominant ethos is one of facilitation rather than of advice-giving or coercion. Most therapies involve one-to-one sessions between client and therapist, but some are conducted with groups, e.g., with families or those who are facing the same traumatic experience, over the phone or via video conferencing. It may be of very brief or long duration, takes place in an organization or private practice setting, and may or may not overlap with medical or other personal welfare.

The therapeutic process is, thus, a talking therapy that allows a client to verbally express deeply what hurts, challenges, or affects the client to develop insights into relating well with self, others, and the environment. The therapeutic process is offered by a psychologist or counselor to help a person (client/patient) facilitate a healthy integration of the influence of childhood experiences on adult life. Therapists are not in business to change clients, to give quick advice, or to solve their problems; instead, they facilitate healing through the process of genuine dialogue with their clients, which will promote change and growth (Corey, 2009, p.6).

Before the work of therapy can begin, an initial bond between therapist and patient needs to be created. E. Bordin (1979) explained that "some basic level of trust surely marks all varieties of therapeutic relationships, but when attention is directed toward the more protected recesses of inner experience, deeper bonds of trust and attachment are required and developed" (p. 254). Researchers who have investigated childhood negative experiences like abuse (physical, sexual, or emotional), neglect, rejection, hatred, isolation, maltreatment, tribal war, or genocide have reported the complex impacts of these experiences on adult functioning (Draucker & Martsolf, 2006, P. 6).

Loken and Reigstad (2012), while working in the field of psychological trauma, discovered that it is important to keep in mind that incidents and situations of childhood adversity are not traumatizing in themselves, but that they are rather potentially traumatizing. In fact, most people who experience such events do not always develop mental health problems (Frueh, Elhai, & Acierno, 2010). Whether or not the individual develops trauma-related problems is dependent upon several characteristics innate to the individual as well as the situation. Hence, they used the term childhood potentially traumatic event (PTE) (pp. 8-9). However, when trauma-related maladjustment exists because of adverse childhood experiences, therapy may facilitate a healthy integration of the adults.

For Instance, childhood adverse and hostile environment, especially sexual abuse, teaches victims that their bodies are not really their own. Victims often report feelings such as shame, fear, depression, and guilt, and many blame themselves for the assault. Some of the emotional and mental challenges of sexual abuse include depression, anxiety, posttraumatic stress, addictions, nightmares, unexplained fear of some places and people, and self-harm. Van der Kolk (2104) explained that exposure therapy could be used for a sexual abuse victim who is afraid to go into the room where the abuse took place or who fears people who wear clothing similar to those worn by an abuser may benefit from such an approach.

Different Approaches/Therapies in Psychology

There are different theories or approaches that a psychologist may utilize in the helping or treatment sessions. They are different angles or lenses through which therapists get into the inner life of the clients to try and trace the problems and ways to help alleviate them (Sommers-Flanagan et al., 2012, p. 9). The major theories are Psychoanalytic theory, Behaviour theory, Cognitive behavioral theory (Cognitive therapy), Humanistic approach (person-centered therapy), Gestalt therapy, Family system therapy, Reality therapy, Integrative therapy, Adlerian therapy, psychospiritual therapy, etc. This chapter will explain them briefly but give more attention to cognitive behavioral therapy and psycho-spiritual therapy.

Psychoanalytic Therapy

The proponent of this theory was Sigmund Freud (1856-1939), a Jew, and the eldest son of his father's second marriage. He was an Austrian neurologist and the father of psychoanalysis, a clinical method for treating psychopathology. The work of Sigmund Freud takes precedence when one thinks of the general idea of helping a client because all the subsequent theories emanated after his, either agreeing or disagreeing with him. It was Freud who first disclosed the fixation and traumatic experiences adults go through because of childhood negative experiences through his five psychosexual developments—oral, anal, phallic, latent, and genital stages when the pleasure-seeking id gets focused on a sexual area or a pleasure zone. A fixation is a persistent focus on an early psychosexual stage (Eysenck, 2004, p. 449). Until this fixation is resolved, the individual will remain stacked in this stage even as an adult. Thus, whatever happens to a child in his/her first six years of life is the determinant factor of the later development of someone's personality.

Freud discovered that some events and desires were often too frightening or painful for his patients to acknowledge, and he believed that such information was locked away in the unconscious mind. This can happen through the process of a defense mechanism called repression. The assumption of Freudian theory is that the unconscious mind governs behavior to a greater degree than people suspect (Ford-Martin, 2001, p. 260). Consequently, the goal of psychoanalysis is to make the unconscious conscious, work with transference, and use interpretation as a tool for therapy and defense mechanisms.

Thus, psychoanalytic therapy focuses on the unconscious factors that motivate human behavior, and attention is given to the first six years of a person's life (Eysenck, 2004). It is by means of the process of free association and dream analysis that a client is helped by the psychoanalyst to explore the unconscious mind and identify repressed memories and feelings to help a person change behavior and overcome problems in desired ways. The techniques are used to access information regarding the client's emotions, shocks, fears, interests, wishes, hostility, fantasies, concerns, and the nature of the experiences of childhood to attain self-empowerment and self-growth.

Behavioral Therapy

Behavior therapy applies the principles of learning to the resolution of specific behavioral disorders. For Corey (2015), the concept of behavior therapy is that clients are not products of their sociocultural sphere but rather products of their environment (pp. 233-234).

In other words, our behavior is basically shaped by the environment, and this can be unlearned. For them, anything learned can be unlearned. The proponents are Ivan P. Pavlov, Edward L. Thorndike, John B. Watson, B. F. Skinner, Albert Bandura, Arnold Lazarus, etc. The basic assumption of the behavioral theory is that a human person is neither good nor bad, but human behavior is governed by basic learning principles, which are shaped by the environment (Corey (2013). Thus, all people are capable of modifying their behaviors under the right circumstances. The therapists are to look at the learned behaviors and how the environment has an impact on those behaviors. For instance, a child who is taught not to stare or look in the eyes of the elders while addressing them but to look down, can relearn how to communicate with proper eye contact.

Humanistic Therapy

Humanistic therapy encourages self-awareness and mindfulness as well as self-exploration that help the client change their state of mind and behavior from one of the reactions to a healthier one. The theory helps the client to believe that all people are inherently good. It adopts a holistic approach to human existence and pays special attention to such phenomena as creativity, free will to choose meaning and value in life, and positive human potential. The person-centered, Client-centered/Patient-Centred therapy of Carl Rogers takes precedence among Humanistic therapists. Using the non-directive approach, the therapist, who is in a congruent state, respects and accepts the incongruent client unconditionally, without judgment or disapproval (unconditional positive regard), listens with empathy, and empowers clients to find answers and ways to improve their life, with the therapist only listening actively and guiding the process. One of the advantages of person-centered therapy is that it has a positive view of an individual and that an individual has the inherent capacity to move toward a state of positive mental health and create their own self-growth given the appropriate circumstances.

This reminds me of the adage of the seed a farmer planted in the garden. When a tiny seed of a mustard tree is planted, it will grow into a mighty tree if given an appropriate condition. This means that the tiny seed has the potential to become a mighty mustard tree. In client-centered therapy, the therapist is like the farmer who plants and waters this tiny mustard seed (clients), providing a nurturing environment where clients can reach their inherent potential. The therapists are there only to provide a positive environment for their clients to experience growth.

Family System Therapy

This therapy sees family as a system that shares similar properties that regulate relationships among parts of the system (Winek, 2009, p.2). The family system seeks to maintain stability through feedback and exploring problems of pathology in the system and helps individuals resolve their problems in the context of their family units, where many issues are likely to begin. Each family member works together with the others to better understand their group dynamic and how their individual actions affect each other and the family unit as a whole. The assumption of the family system therapist is that what happens to one family member may affect everyone in the family. Murray Bowen, an American psychiatrist, is among the major proponents of family system therapy. Bowen believed that the personalities, emotions, and behaviors of grown individuals are a result of their birth order, their role within their family of origin, and the coping mechanisms they have developed for dealing with emotional family issues. To understand the family system, the family must be viewed as a whole (Winek, p.14). Thus, what defines a family is not only the people who make it up but also how they interact with each other to create a unique family dynamic.

Adlerian Therapy

Adlerian therapy is a short-term, goal-oriented, and positive psychodynamic therapy based on the theories of Alfred Adler. The assumption of Adlerian psychology is the belief that people are indivisible; their beliefs and behavior have a purpose and a social meaning. Therefore, an individual is best understood holistically as a total being whose thoughts, feelings, and beliefs are present in a consistent and unified pattern of actions (Carlson and Slavic, 2013, p.1). Adler focused much of his research on feelings of inferiority versus superiority, discouragement, and a sense of belonging in the context of one's community and society at large.

Integrative Therapy

Integrative therapy developed when many psychologists and clinicians used three or four different theories in their practice. Some looked to common elements within all theories, others integrated several theories into one, while some believed in specific treatments for specific issues or symptoms. Integrative therapists are of the view that there is no single approach that can treat each client in all situations. Each person needs to be considered as a whole, and counseling techniques must be tailored to their individual needs and personal circumstances (Okpalaenwe (2014). Thus, integrative psychotherapy refers to the bringing together of the affective, cognitive, behavioral, and physiological systems within a person, with an awareness of the social and transpersonal aspects of the systems surrounding the person (Erskine and Moursund, 2011, p.8).

Psychospiritual Therapy

Many people often turn to religion to seek help and counsel for their daily hassles, which sometimes leads to therapeutic encounters. This is because human beings have always experienced transcendence and mystery at the heart of their existence. Humans are deeply connected with themselves and with the natural world, and this connection also goes beyond self and creation to a transcendence that is a fact of human life. Although our world is secularized, religion is still a factor that influences our day-to-day lives. Sometimes, a person who is spiritual or religious may utilize both fields in the pursuit of healing or well-being. Wald and Calhoun-Brown (2007) explain that while psychotherapy, a model of treatment for mind and body, is considered to be more scientific or medical in approach, spirituality, which encompasses the spirit, mind, and other immeasurable aspects of the body, is generally believed to have little place in the field of psychology.

Certainly, some clinicians are skeptical about the integration of spirituality and therapy, as there is a general fear that this new branch of psychology may be seen as unscientific or invalid (Lindridge, 2008). Many psychologists operate on the belief that religious and spiritual explanations of experience have no place in the study of the mind and behavior because such explanations are neither logical nor material. However, Schermer (2003) contends that the new psycho-spiritual paradigm assumes that many experiences and behaviors do require such explanation because spirituality is the study of the self (p. 29).

Other therapists, however, embrace this new domain and continue to work toward a healthy integration of psychotherapy and spirituality into their practice (Shafranske and Sperry, 2005). However, recently, many research studies have suggested that a therapist's inclusion of an individual's spiritual beliefs may assist in therapy and in the process of healing (Young and Cashwell, 2011, p. 15). Herbert Benson (Benson & Proctor, 1985; Benson & Stark, 1996), a Harvard Physician and a dedicated scientific researcher has obtained rigorous empirical evidence of the health benefits of spiritual practices (Schermer, 2003, p. 25).

As explained above, the etymological root of the word psychotherapy comes from the Greek words *psyche* (soul) and *therapeia* (healing), which means "soul-care" or 'healing of the soul

(Wald and Calhoun-Brown, 2007, p. xxiii). The healing of the soul is a vital and basic need in the life of every human person. This is because human beings are both spiritual beings and matter. The mind, body, and spirit are inseparable realms. Schermer (2003) explains that the soul is the essence of who we are and not an entity that has an existence independent of our body and mind (p. 28). The implication of this "soul-care" is that the task of both psychotherapy and spirituality is to accept and redeem maladjusted human life. In this sense, psychotherapy, when properly practiced, is an inherently spiritual venture.

Psychospiritual therapy, thus, emerged as a way of doing therapy in psychology in order to integrate spiritual principles with psychological models of the mind and behavior (Schermer, 2003, p. 26). Understanding the psychology of spirituality is of tremendous importance to psychotherapy today. This is because spirituality has an integrative and harmonizing function that involves our inner unity, our relationship, and our connectedness with others and to a broader reality (Schneiders, 1998; cf. McGrath, 2006; Nelson, 2009). Spirituality involves a search for higher values, inner freedom, and things that give life meaning (Shannon, 2000, p. 47).

Spirituality is not about religion since even atheists have spirituality. By virtue of being created human, we are already spiritual beings. Humanity is innately possessed by a sense of mystery and awe. William Blake (1698) articulated the view of spirituality over two hundred years ago and viewed all religions as emanating from a common source within. He found spirituality to be present in art, poetry, and other "soulful" expressions of our humanity (quoted in Schermer, 2003, p. 29).

Spirituality is an aspect of our sense of self, a self that is present in nascent form at birth and develops through the life cycle. According to Piedmont (2007), spirituality or the search for the sacred is a universal human potential. It is the capacity to experience self-transcendence and awareness of sacred immanence resulting in greater love for self and others. Spirituality is related to creativity, and it signifies a positive approach, an accepting, embracing, and even loving attitude toward life, suffering, and death (Young and Cashwell, p.18).

Becker (2001) contends that spirituality refers to the soul or the mind and different aspects of human nature that are intangible. Similarly, O'Reilly (2004) defines spirituality as an expression of the transcendent ways in which human potential is fulfilled. Synonyms such as hope, wholeness, meaning, harmony, and transcending (O'Reilly, 2004) are associated with the word spirituality. Schermer, (2003) describes spirituality as that aspect of our psyche that always reaches for union with the mysterious and the beyond (p. 29). This means that spirituality is not a system of belief but a quality of living, being, and experiencing, which involves the awareness of the indescribable and the ineffable.

From these definitions we can deduce that it is in human nature, as a spiritual being, to have a valid experience that transcends the mundane reality. And because the psyche is the totality of the human soul, mind, and spirit, whether conscious or unconscious; it is not separable from spirituality, since our soul is ceaselessly searching for that which is beyond self. In other words, our psyche, being, or essence is not separated from the emotional life, moral health, or intellectual being. Life is connected, and the purpose of each therapy is to enrich life and not just prevent or treat problems. Thus, for psychologists to fully understand a client's issues, they must consider the client's spiritual practice or day-to-day activities that gave rise to spiritual experiences.

Relationship between Psychology and Spirituality

1. Overall wellness and a spiritual worldview are highly compatible because spirituality is an important developmental phenomenon centered on human wellness (Myers and Sweeney, 2008). For each person, the spiritual journey and psychological wellness are about balancing the inner life and the outer world: the mind, soul, and body and interpersonal relationships.
2. Under psychological distress, spiritual coping styles increase. For many, spiritual beliefs play a significant role in their ability to cope with adverse life events. Spiritual practices such as meditation, mindfulness, forgiveness, reconciliation, hope, etc., may offer social and emotional support and help people find meaning and purpose in life (Young & Cashwell, 2011, p. 32; Pargament, 1997).
3. Human suffering has been explored by both psychological scholars and religious scholars, and both have agreed that there is an overlap between their writings on suffering (Young and Cashwell, p. 33). It is clinically astute to use spiritual treatment that works in therapy, e.g., forgiveness as an

aspect of anger management and hope as an important part of treating depression.

Psychospiritual psychology is centered on a spiritual, humanistic, and experiential approach and the use of consciousness (Mijares and Khalsa, 2005, p. 3). Young and Cashwell (2007) enlightened that psychospiritual therapy involves an increased capacity for compassion for others and self, to experience and accept more fully one's pain and suffering and the pain and suffering of others, resulting in a transformation of that suffering into compassion as one becomes transformed (p. 17). Psychospiritual therapy looks at the whole person and journeys inward to the messages and meaning that come from the client's dreams, interactions with others, nature, and the cosmos. The approach is highly relational, created by the dynamic that arises from the encounter between client and therapist, calling on both to be mindful and aware of what is present in the moment.

According to Young and Cashwell, psychospiritual counseling calls the therapist to the following:

- The ability to remain congruent even with one's limitations
- The realization that all human beings are sacred, leading to the experience of awe and wonder in everyday life
- The realization that life has meaning and purpose
- The willingness to take on challenging tasks consistent with one's calling to become a therapist
- The awareness that we are psychologically and spiritually incomplete, broken, and wounded even though we deny this

> fact to others and sometimes to ourselves, but this fact is true for everyone. However, this truth is often affirmed when appropriate and revealed to someone who may offer support (p.7).

Tools for Psychospiritual Approach

The Psychospiritual approach, as an integrative model, utilizes traditional psychological therapeutic skills, such as listening with empathy, questioning, reflecting feelings, using interpretation, responding, paraphrasing, etc., as well as a spiritual approach to support the individual on their journey toward wholeness. This spiritual approach recognizes and accesses higher consciousness using tools such as meditation, imagery, metaphor, visualization, creative arts, awareness, intuition, inner attunement, mindfulness, etc., (Young and Cashwell, 2011). Other tools are Scripture memorization, contemplative prayer, challenging negative thoughts using one's religious resources, religious practices (e.g., gratitude, altruism, and forgiveness), spiritual resources, and involvement in a religious community (Pearce et al. 2015). Both traditional psychotherapy and Psychospiritual therapy work toward a greater understanding of the self in the context of the greater whole.

The cognitive-behavioral therapy or approach (CBT), which will be discussed in detail below, has expanded to include spirituality in its treatment approach. These include, among others: Hayes, et al., (2011), who explored the role of mindfulness principles in the CBT treatment approach; McMinn (2008) in the use of CBT during Christian counseling; Tirch, et al., (2016), who integrated CBT in

Buddhist spirituality; Pearce, et al (2015) in their religiously integrated CBT which they referred to as RCBT. Within these approaches, the therapist utilizes the basic tenets of cognitive-behavioral therapy (CBT) and spiritual values and beliefs to treat the clients (Beitel, Genova, Schuman-Olivier, Arnold, Avants, and Margolin, 2007).

The implication of this scenario is that the client's religious tradition or spirituality is used as a major foundation to identify and replace unhelpful thoughts, values, and behaviors. As a cognitive behavioral therapist who also uses a psychospiritual approach, this work will focus more on how Cognitive Behavioural Therapy (CBT) can be applied in the healing process of wounded religious persons.

Cognitive Behavioural Therapy (CBT)

Cognitive behavioral therapy is a therapeutic approach based on the principle that maladaptive moods and behavior can be changed by replacing distorted or inappropriate ways of thinking with thought patterns that are healthier and more realistic. The word Cognition comes from a Latin word—*cognosco*: "*Con*" which means "with;" *gnosco*, which means "to know." These are from the Greek verb "*nosko*," which means "I know," and the noun is "*gnosis*," which depicts knowledge (Whitfield and Davidson, 2007). Literally it means to know, to conceptualize, to recognize, and to perceive. As the name implies, cognition is the mental process of acquiring knowledge and understanding through the senses, critical thinking, and experiences. It is about the processing of information in the mind, i.e., mental processes, which involve remembering, judging, evaluating, reasoning, problem-solving, and decision-making (O'Donohue and Fisher, 2012).

Human cognition can be conscious and unconscious, concrete, abstract, or intuitive. Szymanska and Palmer (2000) believe that cognitive therapy combines cognitive and behavioral techniques to help individuals modify their moods and behavior by changing their self-defeating thoughts to more realistic and optimistic thoughts (p. 56).

Unlike the other therapies that were greatly influenced by Freud's psychoanalysis, cognitive behavior therapists were influenced more by philosophers rather than by psychologists. For instance, Epictetus, the first-century philosopher suggested that people "are not disturbed by things but by the views which they take of them" (Ellis, 1989, p. 6) Another great influence was Psychiatrist, Alfred Adler, who in his book entitled, "*What Life Should Mean To You*," explained that, "Meanings are not determined by situations, but we determine ourselves by the meaning we give to situations" (Whitfield and Davidson). Another influence was Karen Horney, who talked about the 'tyranny of the should,' which would later influence Albert Ellis' formulation of the "Musturbatory Beliefs Theory." The major proponents of CBT are Albert Ellis, Aaron Beck, and Donald Meichenbaum.

In the 1950s, Albert Ellis developed his Rational therapy. Later, following criticisms that his theory disregarded feelings, in the 1960s and 70s, he renamed it Rational Emotive Therapy (RET). Later, he modified it and called it Rational Emotive Behaviour Therapy (REBT) to incorporate the behavioral component, which critics said was lacking from his theory. In the 1960s, Aaron Beck developed his school of therapy based on the same principles as Ellis, and he called it Cognitive therapy.

Aaron Temkin Beck developed Cognitive Therapy (CT) as a psychiatrist in Pennsylvania. His first book, *Depression: Clinical Experiment and Theoretical Aspect,* was published in 1967/72; while writing this book, he believed that he was mildly depressed, and he found writing this book therapeutic (Dowd, p. 5). He began to develop his theories with observation, and especially his reactions. His theory is about observing the role of information processing in human behavior and behavior change. Working with depressed patients, he found that they experienced streams of negative thoughts that seemed to pop up spontaneously. He called these negative thoughts "Automatic thoughts."

In the 1970s, Donald Meichenbaum also developed his therapy based on similar assumptions as Ellis. His approach was called Cognitive Behaviour Modification.

Assumptions of the CBT Model

The fundamental premise of CBT is that humans are not emotionally disturbed by unfortunate circumstances but by how they construct their views of these circumstances through their language, evaluative beliefs, meanings, and philosophies about the world, themselves, and others (Ellis, 2001). For the CBT model, the way we think affects the way we behave. For them, a human person has the capacity for self-actualization and a propensity for self-destruction through indoctrination and philosophical conditioning.

There are two inherent biological tendencies in humans—the capacity for straight thinking and the capacity for crooked, irrational, or faulty thinking (Corey, 2013). People have a predisposition for self-preservation, happiness, loving communion with others, growth, and self-actualization, but they also have the ability to destroy themselves, avoidance of thought, procrastination, endless repetition of mistakes, superstition, intolerance, perfectionism, and self-blame. Granted that humans are fallible, CBT attempts to help clients accept themselves as creatures who will continue to make mistakes yet, at the same time, learn to live more at peace with themselves (Corey, p. 292).

Contributions of Albert Ellis (1913-2007)

Albert Ellis is an American Psychologist whose Rational Emotive Behaviour Therapy (REBT) insists that blame is at the core of most emotional disturbances (Corey, 2013, 293). For him, if we want to become psychologically healthy, we have to stop blaming ourselves and others and learn to fully and unconditionally accept ourselves despite imperfections. Ellis demonstrates that we have strong tendencies to transform our desires and preferences into dogmatic "shoulds," "musts," and "oughts," demands and commands, which he called *Musturbatory Beliefs*. According to Ellis, our three basic musts or irrational beliefs are:

1. Demand about self: I must do well and win the approval of others, or else I am no good. This leads to anxiety, depression, shame, and guilt, especially when the expectations are not met.
2. Demand about others: Other people must treat me fairly and kindly and how I want them to treat me; if not, they are no good. This leads to feelings like passive aggression, unhealthy anger, rage, acts of violence, etc.
3. Demand about the world and life conditions: I must get what I want when I want it, and I must not get what I don't want, or else life is no good. This belief leads to Self-pity, addictive behavior, problems of self-discipline, and hurt (Corey, 2013, 293).

The ABC Theory of Albert Ellis

Cognitive Behavioural Therapy employs a simple ABC framework that outlines the relationship between events, beliefs, and consequences (Szymanska and Palmer, 2000, 57). Albert Ellis developed the ABC format, which provides a useful tool for understanding the client's feelings, thoughts, events, and behavior (Wolfe, 2007).

A) Activating event or existence of a fact: e.g., I hear the window rattling.

B) Beliefs or thoughts: These are what you tell yourself about the event or your automatic thoughts. For example, when I heard the window rattling, I thought, "Someone is breaking the window."

C) Consequences: These are the effects of how you feel about the event A—(a rattling window), based on your thoughts B—(someone is breaking the window). The response can be emotional, behavioral, or psychological consequences:
   —emotional response: e.g., feeling of anxiety, fear, distress;
   —Behavioural response: Lock the door or call the police;
   —Psychological response: sweating, breathing heavily, shaking, panicking, frightened.
D) Disputing intervention: This involves examining your beliefs and thoughts. Are they realistic? Is it true that someone is breaking the window? Do I have an alternative belief to dispute the automatic thoughts, such as "The wind is blowing hard; that is why the window is rattling?"
E) Effects: This is the new effect of the disputed thoughts, such as calmness and tranquillity. This new effect is possible when my negative thoughts change to more positive thoughts, for instance: "The wind is blowing hard and causes the window to rattle."
F) New Feeling: Peace (Corey, 2013, 293).

The fear (emotional consequence) arises not from the window rattling, but from the negative judgment or appraisal that someone is breaking the window. It could be that the wind is strong and the window is affected (disputing intervention). But because of the negative thoughts, the consequence is fear. However, if the client modifies the belief and thinks that it is the wind that is shaking the window, the new effect and new feeling will be calmness and peace, rather than panic and fear.

From the above example, A, the activating event does not cause C (emotional or behavioral consequences; instead, B (negative thoughts) largely creates C. That is to say that the window-rattling does not create fear or panic. What causes fear and panic is the negative belief (B) that someone is breaking the window. Therefore, between A and C comes B—beliefs about the event. Ellis contends that events are always mediated by beliefs and that emotional consequences of the event are determined by the belief about the event rather than the event itself.

D—Disputing Intervention is the application of methods to help clients challenge their irrational beliefs. Three components are involved in this: detecting, debating, and discriminating.

First, the clients have to detect their irrational beliefs, especially the "shoulds" and the "musts." After detecting this irrational belief, the clients are to debate their dysfunctional belief and learn how to logically question the belief and act against it. Finally, the client learns to discriminate irrational beliefs from a rational one (Corey, p. 294).

Contributions of Aaron Beck

1. Cognitive Triad

The cognitive triad consists of three forms of negative, helpless, or critical thinking that are typical of individuals with depression.

These thoughts are divided into three categories, according to Krapp (2004):

- Negative ideas about self, (I am stupid)
- Negative view of the world, (the world is partial)
- Negative view of the future. (The future is hopeless)

As these three components interact, they interfere with normal cognitive processing, leading to impairments in perception, memory, and problem-solving, with the person becoming obsessed with negative thoughts. Beck explained that the time spent reflecting on negative thoughts would lead patients to treat these thoughts as valid. Beck began helping patients to identify and evaluate these thoughts and found that by doing so, patients could think more realistically, which led them to feel better emotionally and behave more functionally. Beck discovered that frequent negative automatic thoughts reveal a person's core beliefs. These core beliefs are formed over lifelong experiences, and we "feel" these beliefs to be true. E.g., I cannot make friends. That is my nature. (Krapp, 2004).

2. **Negative Self-Schemas**

Unhelpful negative thoughts are acquired from an early individual's childhood when unspoken rules are made in the house (Dowd, 2002). E.g., "You should not talk when the elders are talking. Men should not cry," etc. These laws create a schema, which can be positive or negative. This schema puts a lot of demands and pressure on an individual. Although the schema can help one to act in a certain way that is generally accepted, if the schema is positive; nonetheless, negative schema leads to distorted thinking. Beck believed that depressed individuals develop a negative self-schema, and they possess a set of beliefs and expectations about themselves that are essentially negative and pessimistic (McLeod, 2015).

Beck claimed that negative schemas can also be acquired during childhood as a result of a traumatic event. Experiences that might contribute to negative schemas include:

- Rape of a girl, which can lead to believing that "all men are beasts."
- Death of a parent or sibling.
- Parental rejection, criticism, overprotection, neglect or abuse.
- Bullying at school or exclusion from peer groups.

Apist People with negative self-schemas become prone to making logical errors in their thinking, and they tend to focus selectively on certain aspects of a situation while ignoring equally relevant information (McLeod, 2015).

The nature of maladjustment according to the CBT Model

According to Shamekia (2016), Beck identifies different kinds of cognitive distortions:

1. All-or-nothing thinking, also known as Dichotomous Thinking: This is the tendency to see the situation in terms of polar opposites, e.g., to see oneself as either good or bad. If your performance falls short of perfect, you see yourself as a total failure.
2. Overgeneralization: This involves drawing conclusions from very limited evidence. For instance, a victim of rape who sees all men as beasts.
3. Mental Filter: You pick out a single negative detail and dwell on it exclusively so that your vision of all reality becomes darkened, like the drop of ink that discolors the entire beaker of water.
4. Disqualifying the Positive: When you are told that you are beautiful, you disqualify it with the negative answer: "No, I am not. You are teasing me." In this way, you can maintain a negative belief that is contradicted by your everyday experiences.
5. Jumping into Conclusions: You make a negative interpretation, though there are no definite facts that convincingly support your conclusion. Beck identified two different ways that one could jump to conclusions:

    a. Mind reading: You arbitrarily conclude that someone would always react negatively to you, and you don't bother to test this out.
    b. The Fortune Teller Error: You anticipate that things will turn out badly, and you feel convinced that your prediction is an already-established fact.

6. Magnification (Catastrophizing) or Minimization: You exaggerate the importance of things (such as someone else's achievement), or you inappropriately reduce things until they appear tiny (your desirable qualities or that of the other). This is also called the "binocular trick."

7. Emotional Reasoning: You assume that your negative emotions necessarily reflect the way things really are: "I feel it. Therefore, it must be true."
8. Personalization: This occurs when a person has the tendency to imagine that a situation is attributed to his/her actions. E.g., "Meme did not respond to my greetings because she does not like me." Or "They are looking at me and laughing, therefore, they are laughing at me."

Goals of the Therapy

The goals of the CBT include:

- To identify and modify distorted/thinking errors or negative beliefs in a person in order to improve behavior and life.
- To help depressed people with negative attitudes to work on their disordered lifestyle and resolve their problems.
- To help a client unlearn negative thoughts and negative reactions by teaching them to test their belief system logically, thereby becoming their own therapists.
- Granted that humans are fallible, the therapy attempts to help clients accept themselves as creatures who will continue to make mistakes yet, at the same time, learn to live more at peace with themselves.
- To help clients acquire constructive coping strategies and counteract the negative voices that one cannot achieve success (Szymanska and Palmer, 2000, p. 61).

The Counselling Techniques

Cognitive Behavioural therapists work collaboratively with clients to develop skills for identifying and working on distorted thoughts and beliefs. The client must first set goals, which the therapist will examine to ensure that the goals are specific, measurable, achievable, realistic, and time-bound (SMART) (Szymanska and Palmer, p. 62). According to Szymanska and Palmer, there are two techniques for therapy: Cognitive and Behavioural Techniques.

Cognitive techniques are used to help the client identify, evaluate, and modify negative automatic thoughts, while behavioural techniques serve to help clients test their negative automatic thoughts. These techniques are explained below:

The Cognitive Technique

1. Cognitive Restructuring

One of the techniques of CBT in helping clients modify their negative thoughts is the use of cognitive restructuring (Ellis 2008). This is a technique of cognitive therapy that teaches clients how to improve themselves by replacing irrational beliefs with rational beliefs. Restructuring involves helping clients learn to monitor their self-talk, identify maladaptive self-talk, and substitute it with healthy thoughts in order to arrive at a new feeling "F." However, the client has to choose to examine, challenge, modify, and uproot B—the irrational belief. Cognitive restructuring is a very powerful technique that has been adapted to help people cope with all manner of stressful events and conditions. One drawback of this technique is that it is somewhat difficult for people to learn it in a self-help mode without the assistance of a therapist (Corey, 2013, p. 296). However, the goal of cognitive restructuring is to enable people to replace stress-induced thinking habits with more accurate and less stress-induced thinking habits.

2. Questioning

Here the therapist uses the Socratic method of questioning to challenge irrational, unhelpful, and negative beliefs so that the client will become aware of them. For instance, the therapist can ask: "Supposing you are taking an evening walk around your neighborhood. And there are steps behind you. When you look back, you see two men behind you. What thoughts come into your mind? Maybe: "Oh my goodness, I am going to be robbed." Where is this thinking coming from? What are the effects of this thinking? Probably, fear, anxiety, panic, etc. Are there alternative ways of looking at these men? Can you see them as people going for an evening walk as well? What are the effects of this alternative thinking? Perhaps, a feeling of relief and peace." This questioning may help a client avoid jumping to a negative conclusion when the situation arises.

3. Active listening

This is when the therapist makes a conscious effort to listen to the client with undivided attention (attending) in order to hear not only the words that the client is saying but also to listen to the non-verbal behavior. Active and empathic listening will help a therapist respond to the client with open-ended questioning, reflecting on feelings, challenging skills, summarizing skills, and paraphrasing the client's point of view in order to demonstrate that the therapist is actively present for the client.

4. Auto-suggestion

Clients use this method to rehearse and talk to themselves in a role-play manner about real-life situations. For instance, they tell themselves in a private setting, "Yes, I can."

5. Distraction/thought stopping

This exercise helps the client stop thinking negatively. When clients have a negative thought, they can stop and count back from 100 in threes, i.e., 100, 97, 94, 91, 88, etc.; read interesting books or recall pleasant experiences in detail.

6. Double standard method

Since some people tend to be harder on themselves than on their friends or colleagues, clients are asked to treat themselves as they would treat a friend in the same situation.

7. Disadvantages and advantages

This is where clients are asked to write the merits and demerits of holding their negative thoughts.

8. Dealing with emotional reasoning

Clients are advised not to confuse feelings with facts. When a person does not feel good enough, they can be asked: "Is there evidence that you are not good enough?"

9. Looking for another explanation

This is seeking alternative explanations for a situation. For instance, rather than thinking that the novice director was angry at the formee because of not responding to the novice's greetings, the novice is asked to consider another alternative. "Could it be that the novice director was having a quiet day of prayer?"

10. Testing out the validity of the automatic thoughts

This is where a client is asked to test out their new beliefs using behavioral experiments. E.g.: "If you think you cannot swim, enter the water first."

11. Eliciting schema and underlying assumption

E.g., Client: "If I cannot do my job well, I am useless."

Counsellor: "Does it mean that if you cannot do your job well, you are useless?"

Here, "I am useless" is the eliciting schema. This is not about doing the job well but rather about the negative thoughts. The client and the therapist can work on modifying it.

12. Giving homework:

Clients are asked to keep track of their feelings and how they relate to their thoughts, as well as to indicate experiences that suggest that these feelings are not completely true. The client is encouraged to write down a new and more realistic belief and rate the confidence the client has in the new belief on a regular basis (Szymanska and Palmer, pp. 63-64).

Behavioral Techniques

1. **Relaxation exercises**: This is a form of cognitive distraction that calms the mind and body and helps clients control their physiological responses to stress. For instance, when you feel sad, sit down, relax, take a deep breath a couple of times, and think of the time you were appreciated for your great creativity.
2. **Systematic desensitization or Graded Exposure**: This technique helps clients face their fears step by step, starting with the least item that causes anxiety. For instance, a rubber snake can be used for someone who is afraid of snakes to desensitize the fear of the snake little by little. The same will be

applicable to someone who has a phobia of height. The client can begin by climbing a very insignificant height until the client progresses to a higher one.

3. **Assertiveness or social skill training**: One who thinks negatively about self and lacks assertiveness can be given the opportunity to address the public in a social gathering in order to build self-confidence (Szymanska and Palmer, pp. 63-64).

Strength or the contribution of CBT

- The therapy has provided a manual for treatment, especially the treatment of depression, anxiety disorder, substance abuse, couples problems, suicidal behavior, phobias, bipolar disorder, eating disorders, drug abuse, anxiety disorders, schizophrenia, and personality disorder.
- The Beck Depression Inventory is very helpful for themes that cause depression, deprivation, loss, defeat, or the feeling of failure. Cognitive therapy has been very effective for treating depression (Hollon and Beck, 1994), and moderately effective for anxiety problems (Beck, 1993).
- The Beck Hopelessness Scale is found to be predictive of eventual suicide. It is used for measuring suicide intent and behavior and to identify hopelessness as the key psychological variable and as a suicide risk factor (Leahy, 2003, p. 6).
- Beck discovered the treatment strategies for various anxiety disorders. In his research in 1980, he looked at the importance of negative cognition in perpetuating anxiety. Clients were taught to challenge such beliefs and to improve their coping abilities by recognizing their resources.

- The therapy focuses on teaching self-counseling skills to cope with daily stress.
- It has had success in treating phobias through a technique called exposure therapy that involves gradual exposure to the object of fear; for instance, using a rubber snake to help those who have a phobia of snakes.

Weaknesses and Limitations of CBT

- It is criticized for being non-historical in nature, whereby only the current causes of irrational thinking and dysfunctional cognition are examined and changed. It does not address the possible underlying causes of mental health conditions, such as an unhappy childhood. (Thomas Dowd, 2002, p.18). As Beck extends his cognitive therapy to personality disorders, he modifies his theory to take into account developmental histories and the cognitive distortions arising from the early stages of development.
- Due to the structured nature of CBT, it may not be suitable for people with more complex mental health needs.
- In CBT, too much attention is given to the cognition part of life.
- It sees a client as a student who should learn how to fix a negative thought.
- CBT focuses on the individual's capacity to change themselves (their thoughts, feelings, and behaviors) and does not address wider problems in systems or families that often have a significant impact on an individual's health and well-being.

Although cognitive therapists concentrate on the negative thoughts of a person, they still believe that many factors contribute to the development of dysfunctional cognition. These include people's biological and genetic dispositions, life experiences, and the accumulation of knowledge and learning (Seligman and Reichenberg, 2014, p. 295). Therefore, distorted cognition begins to take shape in childhood and is reflected in adults' fundamental beliefs and schemas because the thoughts are already biased and distorted.

Ultimately, all the different approaches used for the therapeutic process vary somewhat. However, they can all result in similar outcomes—helping clients function effectively in society. And because a single approach to psychotherapy does not always provide the best benefit to the client, therapists, who are trained in one particular therapeutic model, such as psychoanalytic, cognitive, behavioral, family, or gestalt therapy, are often encouraged to use tools borrowed from other therapies to come up with a unique and effective form of treatment that is suitable and effective for the individual client. This chapter has briefly explored some psychological therapies used in the helping process, the next chapter will summarise and conclude the work.

CHAPTER SIX

Summary and Recommendations

"We are never defeated unless we give up on God."

—Ronald Reagan

This chapter summarizes the study's findings and presents recommendations to help consecrated individuals cope with the impact of childhood experiences as they mature in faith and relate within their communities.

Summary of the Findings

Evidence from the stories of men and women interviewed in this work supports concerns that childhood experiences of parental care or neglect can impact a child's development. This is in line with the psychodynamic theory of Freud, Erikson's psychosocial development theory, and Fowler's faith development theory. As explained above, Erikson (1963) believes that consistency, reliability, and sameness are important values for a child, so that the child can learn to trust self and rely on the providers (p. 287). When the love of the mother or the significant other is lacking, then the child will feel insecure and develop a lack of trust in the significant other and the world around him/her.

While many religious persons who were interviewed experienced a loving and caring childhood environment, many of them did not have this consistency of love and, therefore, didn't experience a healthy passage from childhood to adulthood. Some are affected by physical, emotional, or sexual abuse; others are affected by war, genocide, political clashes, rejection of parents, divorce of parents, death of parents, neglect, and a very strict disciplinary environment. The question is: How effectively are parents fulfilling their responsibilities in raising their children? The Book of Proverbs expresses it well: "Teach children the right way, and they will not stray from it when they are old" (22:6).

The saying "Tell me your parents, and I can predict your behavior" suggests that a person's behavior can be influenced by their parents. Some parents are preoccupied with work, business, education, or other pursuits, leaving their children in the care of nannies, older siblings, friends, or relatives who may not be positive influences. Some parents worry when their children are on school vacation. Instead of spending quality time with them, they send them off to another holiday education program. Sometimes, working parents or absent parents do not notice the fear and pain in their children's eyes, which is expressed through non-verbal gestures. Unfortunately, little girls have been raped when their parents were away and entrusted them to the care of older adults, siblings, or relatives.

Our families are responsible for not only reproducing children but also socializing them. Parents, siblings, and significant others in the family are role models and counselors of behavior for children. The family is the primary influence on a child's behavior, success in life, and development of coping abilities and faith in oneself, others, and God. When families neglect their responsibilities as the child's first educators, it can negatively impact the child's social life.

The research findings show that individuals with consistent love and care reported good self-esteem and self-confidence, a fulfilled and joyful consecrated life, the ability to cope with life challenges, positive religious faith development, the ability to take up roles, deeper relationships with God, a deeper prayer life, and a joyful presence in the community.

It was discovered that many religious persons who have a healthy passage from childhood to adulthood are very consistent in their religious values and vowed life. Most of them adopted the religious belief of their parents and they are happy and value their religious life. Many were introduced to faith when they were young. Their significant others taught them how to pray and got them engaged in parish activities. Some of them are highly placed in the congregation and some are leaders of their congregation.

The results from this work also revealed that many consecrated persons with a history of childhood maltreatment and neglect reported lower levels of self-esteem/self-confidence, incessant anger, depression, loneliness, bitterness, suicidal thoughts, insecure attachment, arrogance, prejudice, bullying of community members, as well as inappropriate coping behavior, etc. Some coping skills discovered in this work include alcohol abuse, bullying, passive aggression, and addiction to social media. This is consistent with the findings of Mvungu (2014) as explained above that family characteristics such as poor parental supervision, parental violence, and abuse, low parental involvement with the child, parental aggression, including erratic or harsh parental discipline, a difficult economy, as well as antisocial parents have been found to greatly contribute to behavior maladjustment in children, which leads to inefficacy coping response of alcohol and substance abuse, and violence in the child.

Thus, this careful analysis reveals the devastating effects of negative childhood experiences on some religious men and women. Sometimes, these experiences are hidden in religious garments and are not easily apparent to outsiders. The ugly thing is that some religions seek the solution to their problems through other means, such as witchcraft practices (Gitau, 2016) and addictions to phones and social media. Gitau explains: "We have to pay close attention to the phenomenon of witchcraft in our religious communities.... It is an urgent matter that needs to be addressed today. We have quite a number of consecrated men and women who experience inner insecurity" (p. 144). Seeking solutions through witchcraft when one experiences psychological or spiritual problems is already a betrayal of a belief in God.

Using alcohol, social media, phones, etc., as balms to briefly soothe and relieve wounds, pains, loneliness, and insecurity that we feel will never solve the problem of our restless hearts. Our wounded and restless hearts can only find rest in God, says St. Augustine of Hippo, and in seeking help. This reminded me of a story told by a parish priest in a certain parish during the homily on a Sunday Mass.

> A religious person once had a dream. In that dream, she was late for Mass because she was chatting with a friend on the phone. After the Mass, the parishioners normally have an adoration of the Blessed Sacrament. When the priest who had finished celebrating Mass left for the sacristy to remove

his vestments, he asked the nun to expose the Blessed Sacrament for adoration. The nun hesitated and agreed finally. When the dismissal song was over, she approached the tabernacle and opened it. A large television screen fell from the tabernacle and she was able to grab it before it broke. She put it on the floor and wondered how a large-screen television set was able to fit into a tiny tabernacle. The next things that fell off from the tabernacle were two big smartphones. She also kept them on the floor. The next was a big bundle of money. And finally, after removing the money, she was able to see at the back corner of the tabernacle was a very tiny monstrance with a tiny consecrated host.

Because a dream's message is about the dreamer, her spiritual guide asked her to explain the place of Jesus in her life. She confessed that she was addicted to three things: Television programs, her phones, and her insatiable appetite for money and material things. These three things occupied her life so much that she had tiny or no space for Jesus or for a deeper prayer life.

This story is the unfortunate dilemma of many of us in religious life. Jesus' place in our lives has become very insignificant. His place and love are replaced by love for material things. Some religious are so busy chasing after material things, investments, and personal security that they have little or no time for prayer or a relationship with Jesus. Others are so lonely in the community of many members that they take solace in social media. We need to adhere to Sawubona's philosophy, as explained above. Our interconnectedness, presence to one another, and the culture of encounter are important aspects of a supportive community living. When we don't look out for one another, some members could be isolated. Desmond Tutu (2004) once said, "A person is a person through other persons. None of us comes into the world fully formed. We would not know how to think, walk, speak, or behave as human beings unless we learned it from other human beings. We need other human beings to be human" (pg. 25).

The stories in this work clearly demonstrate the brokenness and wounds present in consecrated life. However, there is still hope, as these wounded individuals can be helped through therapy or spiritual direction. Therapy or counseling sessions aim to help religious individuals function effectively. One participant puts it well: "A healed religious person, will become an effective religious. We all need healing because we are wounded."

After completing the interview, it was obvious that therapy or spiritual direction is for every individual whether we have a healthy passage of childhood life or not. According to Freud, some amount of fixation is inevitable because of insufficient or excessive gratification. This is because when a child feels too comfortable and gets attached to a certain stage, moving to another phase might result in distress and frustration, hence fixation (Ellis et al., 112). And since, according to Erikson, cited in Schultz and Schultz (2009), personality development is an ongoing process throughout life, it is imperative to have opportunities for ongoing growth among religious people, no matter their stage of formation, because the challenges of life can be overwhelming.

Recommendations

More than 70% of those interviewed recommended that congregations should include counseling as part of the initial formation curriculum in order to facilitate the transformative formation process. This will help formees process their wounds before they start formation and thus become integrated consecrated persons eventually. Certainly, there will be no spiritual growth or maturity among religious persons without healthy emotional and psychological maturity.

Another recommendation from the participants is to train formators in some counseling skills so that they will be well-equipped for the work of formation. Sending them to a formation program is not enough for their ministry at this age and time.

It is necessary to create an enabling environment for those who desire to be counseled to trust the process. Sometimes formators seek to know what the formees shared with the therapist. This affects the ethical value of confidentiality, and the formees might end up not opening up to the process or choosing what to share with the therapist. Thus, the formee keeps the most challenging experiences for fear that the formator might get to hear his/her story.

Another recommendation is for religious to become conversant with Fowler's instruments for measuring faith. Some religious Congregations only use psychological and behavioral assessments when recruiting new members. It will benefit congregations to include instruments developed by Fowler during this recruitment period to ascertain how the faith of these aspirants developed, their prenatal and postnatal developments, who were the people who inspired faith in them, and how it was transmitted. These questions and more will help formators understand the formee and how to help them in their faith journey. Some of the instruments developed by Fowler for measuring faith include the Faith Development Interview (FDI), Faith Styles Scales (FSS), and Faith Development Scale (FDS).

Other instruments that will help wounded religious in going through the journey of healing are the Beck Depression Inventory, which can help depressed religious persons monitor depression, deprivation, or the feeling of failure, and the Beck Hopelessness Scale, which measures suicide intent and behavior and may identify hopelessness in a religious person.

Conclusion

The journey toward wholeness is essential for all religious individuals who have been wounded by childhood experiences. This book sheds light on how positive and/or negative childhood experiences can impact the faith development of consecrated individuals, and how those who have been wounded can begin their journey toward wholeness. The study found that positive parental care and religious practices during childhood foster a strong religious faith and healthy coping mechanisms in adults. On the other hand, childhood neglect and abuse can negatively impact adults, leading to unhealthy coping skills. The study supports the fact that childhood trauma can have a lasting impact on religious individuals. If this concept holds true for some consecrated men and women, it would be appropriate to ensure that consecrated persons receive adequate therapy at the beginning of their formation process and even during their ongoing formation process. When individuals affected by trauma do not engage in therapeutic processes, receive spiritual guidance, or find healing through prayer, they may never fully recover from their traumatic experiences.

Epilogue

"Although the life of a person is in a land full of thorns and weeds, there is always a space in which the good seed can grow. You have to trust God."

—Pope Francis

Sr. Maris (not her real name) clashed with one of her sisters on almost everything. Previously, Maris was the best-behaved young sister among the members of her community until Sr. Stella (not her real name) joined the community. The members of the community believed that Stella might be the one with the problem since Maris had been a wonderful community member. They attributed the conflict between Maris and Stella to a personality clash and recommended help.

During this process, Maris discovered that the verbal, emotional, and physical abuse by her mother was impacting her adult relationship. Her mother would often compare her to her siblings. As a result, Maris grew up believing she was worthless and unintelligent. Her mother would also physically punish her for minor mistakes using a large stick or a leather belt. This corporal punishment, combined with verbal and emotional abuse, caused Maris to develop a deep hatred for her mother, leading to her becoming rude, stubborn, and discourteous.

Life was good for Maris in this community until her childhood wounds resurfaced with the arrival of Stella in their community. This could be possible because Stella reminded her of her mother, and unfortunately, they shared the same name. Maris transferred her hatred for her mother to her sister, who now happened to be the new local superior. When Maris was instructed by her new leader to perform a task in the community, she would intentionally do the opposite just to upset her. Maris admitted that she felt satisfied when she succeeded in frustrating Stella. With therapy and the grace of God, the healing process began, and Maris became aware of her transference and realized that Stella was not her mother. Today, they have a better relationship as Maris continues her healing process.

This is a typical example of how childhood experiences can impact a religious person. One can only imagine what she could become if this wound is not addressed. Maybe, a wounded, negative, and probably a bitter religious. Maybe a bully, an insecure person with a low self-image. Sometimes, the journey of healing and wholeness is incredibly challenging, akin to passing through a fiery furnace. It is a painful, scary, and shameful journey that we fear. Nevertheless, a tree can actually bear much fruit only after pruning it (Jn. 15:1-2). Gold could only become flashy and golden after going through a torture by fire. The Book of Sirach says: "Gold is tested by fire, and human character is tested in the furnace of humiliation" (2:5-7; 1 Pt.1:7). Sometimes passing through this fire of healing brings much darkness and "why me" questions. It brings much loneliness; it is muddy, messy, unclear, and mucky; and it is very cold because it is a journey one travels alone through God's grace and the guidance of a therapist/spiritual director.

Paul Berchtold tells a story of a seed buried in the mud:

Once upon a time, a seed was buried in the mud after falling on the ground. Then it rained a little. And a deer came along and stepped on it and pushed it deep in the mud. It was in darkness. It was cold and wet. It shivered. It was just plain no fun. It was icky. It was dirty. It was muddy. It was mucky. It was stuck in the mud. Life just wasn't fair. It was all alone. If only it had fallen like the other seeds: on the grass or on the log over there or at least not been stepped on.

But what the little seed did not see was the mouse that ate the seeds on the grass, the bird that ate the seeds on the log, and the chipmunk that gathered the seeds on the ground to store and eat all winter long.

It couldn't see this because it was stuck in the mud. It didn't know how lucky it was. Now, besides being squished tight in the mud, it was also locked in its shell. It tried to get out of its terrible predicament, but it could not. As the autumn days got shorter and shorter, it got colder and colder too. It went through a terribly cold and dark winter.

Finally, after what seemed forever, slowly, the days grew a little longer, a little warmer. The seed had work to do. It began to grow. The water in the mud had softened its shell. Still, it was hard to get out of its shell. It exerted energy like never before. Finally, it broke free. Then it used more energy to go not up, but down, struggling to send a tiny little root through that compacted mud–it needed something to hold on to. Then, it had to struggle again to send a tiny shoot to the warm sunlight above.

You would think its troubles were over. Not so fast. In a whole year, it grew only a few inches, while other plants grew by leaps and bounds as if to mock the little seed. Every autumn, it lost its leaves. In winter, it barely survived, covered with snow. And as it got a little taller, it had to go through windstorms and snow storms.

But one thing was peculiar. Even while it slowly grew up to the sunny blue sky, it never forgot its roots. It had the wisdom to keep growing its roots deeper and deeper in the mud. In fact, it used every wind storm, every blizzard, every shaking, and every vibration to wiggle its roots deeper and deeper into the black icky mud. It realized that it had been protected and helped by the mud–it did not want to let go.

The years rolled by, and the seasons, too. Each summer, it slowly but surely grew. Each winter, it became a little tougher and stronger. It had little joys and little sorrows throughout its life, like all of us do. Then, the fiercest of all storms came. The wind blew so violently, that trees all around were dashed to the ground, broken, uprooted, a jangled mess. After the devastation, the sun shone once again. It had lost some leaves, quite a few, in fact, but that would soon be remedied. It was still standing! And because it had made good under every condition, it stood there in all its glory. It had become a mighty oak tree.

Ultimately, the buried seed realized two things: All problems come with lessons, and rather than focusing on the wound sustained through life experiences, it is better to remain positive and hopeful.

Secondly, the attitude of thankfulness is the key. We ought to be grateful for who we are and for what we are becoming. Each one of us is like a seed in the mud, ready to grow into that mighty oak tree. However, we have to endure the painful experience of being spiritually, psychologically, socially, physically, and emotionally pruned, as well as enduring being tested by fire before we are healed, rather than getting stuck in the mud.

Inasmuch as we seek healing and wholeness through therapy, we are also to be aware that the greatest healer is Christ himself and have faith in his promises. For according to him, "I came that they may have life, and have it more abundantly" (Jn. 10:10). In another place, Jesus says: "The Spirit of the Lord is upon me because he has anointed me to bring good news to the poor. He has sent me to proclaim release to the captives and recovery of sight to the blind, to let the oppressed go free" (Lk. 4:18). Ultimately, authentic healing comes from Christ, who is able to release us from the bondage of childhood trauma and all its adverse influence.

We must also never forget that one of the best things about the wounds we carry is that, as we receive healing, we can learn to become wounded healers (Carl Jung and Henri Nouwen) and comforters of others. St. Paul puts it well in 2 Cor. 1:3-4: "Blessed be the God and Father of our Lord Jesus Christ, the Father of compassion and the God of all comfort, who comforts us in all our troubles, so that we can comfort those in any trouble with the same comfort we ourselves have received from God."

In fact, it is not unusual that our reaching out to help and comfort others is the very path God chooses to comfort us, especially during dark moments.

A story was told of an orphan girl who was about to be married. She was attractive and one of the most capable girls in the institution. One day, sores began to appear on her hands, and it was determined that she had leprosy.

She was removed from the orphanage and sent to the leper asylum. She was dressed in beautiful white garments as she walked into that awful place, accompanied by her brother. The women there looked sad and hopeless. When the girl saw them, she buried her head on her brother's shoulder and wept, "My God, am I going to become as they are?" She was so distressed that those around her were afraid she might harm herself.

Those who were in charge of the leper asylum sympathized with her and asked her if she wouldn't like to help those poor women. A ray of hope came to her and she began to see the possibilities that lay ahead. She started a school and taught the women to sing, read, and write. She could play the organ, so one was bought for her. Gradually a change took place. The houses were made clean, neat, and tidy; the women washed their clothes and combed their hair, and that once horrible place was transformed.

After being there for some time, she said, "When I came to the asylum, I doubted the love of God. Now I know that God had work for me to do, and if I had not become a leper, I would never have discovered that work. Every day I live, I thank God for sending me here and teaching me to care for others."

Sometimes, when we are wounded, we join the band of negative people, and our daily songs are: "Poor me!" "Why me?" The truth about self-pity is that it is addictive. It's like a drug, and soon, we barely even notice that we are playing the game of self-pity. We remain so negative that we console ourselves with different kinds of addictions, get stuck in the mud, and become grumpy. During a workshop in January of 2024, a religious sister asked Fr. Ron Rolheiser (OMI), a theologian and an author of many books, including *The Holy Longing: Guidelines for a Christian Spirituality*: "Why are some older religious persons grumpy and agitated?" Fr. Ron responded: "It is not an older religious who is grumpy; it is a grumpy person who is aging." God wants us to experience joy and live a fulfilled life. Life may not be perfect, but it is worth enjoying.

Pope Francis says: "Life is a journey. When we stop, things don't go right." Do not stop where you have fallen or where your childhood experiences have taken you. Get up and get going! You can't keep trouble from coming, but you needn't give it a chair to sit in. When we become negative and pitch our tents with negative people, we stop growing and focus on our wounds. Nonetheless, positive people will keep advancing on the journey to wholeness no matter how many times they have fallen. When other consecrated persons with positive thinking are advancing, sometimes we try to pull them down with our pettiness and negative attitude. The best reaction is not to fight those who are pulling you down, because to fight them, you need to step down to the muddy level of their lives and become like them. Do not allow negative people to drag you into their mud.

Pope Francis, on 20th September 2017, during a general audience at St. Peter's Square in the Vatican, was enumerating "how to have hope" to the young people. He said:

> "Wherever you are, build! When life gets hard, and you have fallen, get up. Never stay down. Get up and let people help you to your feet. If you're sitting, start walking! Start the journey. Nothing is more human than making mistakes, and these mistakes must not become a prison for you. The son of God came "not for the healthy, but for the sick." So, people should not be afraid to get up again and start over when they fall because God is your friend. If you're bored stiff, crush boredom with good works. If you feel empty and demoralized, ask if the Holy Spirit may newly replenish that void. Don't listen to those who spread hatred and division. Don't make room for bitter or dark thoughts. Spend time with people who have kept a child-like heart."

When we continue to wallow in self-pity and blame our circumstances on people who caused our pain, we will never experience healing. When we think negatively, we tend to act accordingly. If we surround ourselves with pessimistic people, we are more likely to have a negative outlook on life. When we surround ourselves with forward-thinking people or maintain a positive mindset, we become hopeful and act with optimism. Therefore, the ability to grow and heal is in our hands. The power to experience happiness or sadness is in our hands. The power to succeed or not is in our hands. The power to think positively or negatively is in our hands. The power to journey to wholeness or not is in our hands.

High in the Himalayan Mountains lived a wise old man. Periodically, he ventured down into the local village to entertain the villagers with his special knowledge and talents. One of his skills was psychically telling the villagers the contents of their pockets, boxes, or minds.

A few young boys from the village decided to play a joke on the wise old man and discredit his special abilities. One boy devised the idea to capture a bird and hide it in his hands. He knew, of course, that the wise old man would know the object in his hands was a bird. The boy devised a plan. Knowing the wise old man would correctly state the object in his hands was a bird, the boy would ask the old man if the bird was dead or alive. If the wise man said the bird was alive, the boy would crush the bird in his hands so that the bird would be dead when he opened his hands. But, if the wise man said the bird was dead, the boy would open his hands and let the bird fly free. So, no matter what the old man said, the boy would prove the old man a fraud.

The following week, the wise old man came down from the mountain into the village. The boy quickly caught a bird and cupping it out of sight in his hands, walked up to the wise old man and asked, "Old man, old man, what is it that I have in my hands?" The wise old man said, "You have a bird, my son." And he was right. The boy then asked, "Old man, old man, tell me: Is the bird alive or is it dead?" The wise old

> man looked at the boy, thought for a moment, and said, "The bird is as you choose it to be" (Hyatt, 2011).

And so, it is with our lives. The power is in our hands to give in to self-pity. God has given us a great gift—our lives. What will you do with yours? Will you live an intentional life, filled with joy even in the midst of pain and trauma? Or will you be influenced by adverse childhood experiences that have colored your adult life and affected your behavior? The power is in your hands!

References

Adelson, E. & Shapiro, V. (1987). "Ghosts in the Nursery: A Psychoanalytic Approach to the Problems of Impaired Infant-Mother Relationships." In Fraiberg, L. (Ed.) *Selected Writings of Selma Fraiberg*, (pp. 101-136). Columbus, Ohio State University Press.

Albom, M. (2007). *Tuesdays With Morrie: An Old Man, A Young Man, And Life's Greatest Lesson.* New York: Doubleday.

American Counselling Association (2014) "2014 ACA Code of Ethics as Approved by the ACA Governing Council." Retrieved from https://www.counseling.org.

American Psychological Association (2010). "Ethical Principles of Psychologists and Code of Conduct." Retrieved from www.apa.org/ethics/code.

Andrade, A. (2014). Using Fowler's Faith Development Theory in Student Affairs Practice. *College Student Affairs Leadership*, 1(2). Retrieved from http://scholarworks.gvsu.edu/csal/vol1/iss2/2.

Andreou. E. (2001). Bully/Victim Problems and their Association with Coping Behaviour in Conflictual Peer Interactions among School-Age Children. *Educational Psychology*, 21, 59-66.

Asadoorian, M. O., & Kantarelis, D. (2005). *Essentials of Inferential Statistics*, 4th Edition. Lanham, MD: University Press of America, Inc.

Avery, W.O. (1990). A Lutheran Examines James W. Fowler. *Religious Education*, 85(1), 69-83.

Bandura, A. (1977). *Social Learning Theory*. Englewood Cliffs, NJ: Prentice Hall.

Bandura, A. (1986). *Social Foundations of Thought and Action: A Social Cognitive Theory*. New Jersey: Prentice-Hall, Inc.

Banyard, P., & Flanagan, C. (2009). *Ethical Issues & Guidelines in Psychology*. New York: Routledge.

Batson, D. (1982). *Religion and the Individual*. New York: Oxford University Press.

Bazeley, P. (2012). Integrative Analysis Strategies for Mixed Data Sources. *American Behavioural Scientist,* 56(6), 814-828.

Beale, A.V. (2001). Bully busters: Using Drama to Empower Students to Take a Stand against Bullying Behaviour. *Professional School Counselling,* 4, 300-306.

Becker, D. M. (2001). Integrating Behavioural and Social Sciences with Public Health. In N.

Schneiderman, M. A. Speers, J. M. Silvia, H. Tomes & J. H. Gentry (Eds.), *Public Health and Religion* (pp. 351- 368). Washington, DC: American Psychological Association.

Beitel, M., Genova, M., Schuman-Olivier, Z., Arnold, R., Avants, K. S., & Margolin, A. (2007).

Reflections by Inner-City Drug Users on a Buddhist-Based Spirituality-Focused Therapy: A Qualitative Study. *American Psychological Association,* 77(1), 1-9.

Bellamy, J., Mou, S., & Castle, K. (2004). Social Influences upon Faith Development. *The*

National Church Life Survey (NCLS) Research Occasional Paper, no. 5. Retrieved from file:///C:/Users/admin/Desktop/Research%20Work/Fowler/NCLSOccasionalPaper5-SocialInfluencesuponFaithDevelopment.pdf.

Benjamin Jr, L. T., DeLeon, P. H., Freedheim, D. K., & VandenBos, G. R. (2003). Psychology as a Profession. In Donald K. Freedheim & Irving B. Weiner (Eds), *Handbook of Psychology Vol. 1, History of Psychology*. (pp. 27-46). New Jersey: John Wiley & Sons, Inc.

Berchtold, P. (2011). "A Gratitude Story." Retrieved from https://mygratitudelife.wordpress.com/2011/12/28/day-359-a-gratitude-story-the-seed-in-the-mud/.

Bierman, A. (2005). The Effects of Childhood Maltreatment on Adult Religiosity and Spirituality: Rejecting God the Father Because of Abusive Fathers? *Journal of the Scientific Study of Religion*, 44(3), 349-359.

Blaxter, L., Hughes C., & Tight, M. (2006). *How to Research,* 3rd Edition. New York: Open University Press.

Blocher, D. H. (2000). *The Evolution of Counselling Psychology.* New York: Springer Publishing Company.

Boeree, G. C. (2006). "Personality Theories: Erik Erikson." Psychology Department, Shippensburg University. Shippensburg, PA: Retrieved from http://www.social-psychology.de/do/pt_erikson.pdf.

Bowlby, J. (1969). *Attachment and Loss.* Volume I: Attachment. London: The Hogarth press.

Bowlby, R. P. L., Bowlby, R. J. M., & Gaitling, A. (1988). *John Bowlby: A Secure Base: Clinical Application of Attachment Theory.* New York: Routledge.

Boyatzis, R. (1998). *Transforming Qualitative Information: Thematic Analysis and Code Development.* Thousand Oaks, CA: Sage.

Bridges, L. J., & Moore, K. A. (2002). *Religion and Spirituality in Childhood and Adolescence.* Child Trends. Retrieved from https://www.childtrends.org/wp-content/uploads/2002/01/Child_Trends-2002_01_01_FR_ReligionSpiritAdol.pdf.

British Association for Counsellors and Psychotherapy (2013). "Ethical Framework for Good Practice in Counselling and Psychotherapy." Retrieved from www.bacp.co.uk/ethical_framework/personal.php.

British Psychological Society (2009). *Code of Ethics and Conduct.* Leicester, England: The British Psychological Society Press.

Brownell, P. (2010). *Gestalt Therapy: A Guide to Contemporary Practice.* New York: Springer.

Busby, D. M., Walker, E. C., & Holman, T. B. (2011). The Association of Childhood Trauma with Perceptions of the Self and Partner in Adult Romantic Relationships. *Personal Relationships,* 18(4), 547–561.

Bruwer, B., Govender, R., Bishop, M., Williams, D. R., Stein, D. J. & Seedat, S. (2013). Association between Childhood Adversities and Long-Term Suicidality among South Africans from the Results of the South African Stress and Health Study: A Cross-

Sectional Study. Retrieved from http://bmjopen.bmj.com/content/4/6/e004644.

Bwisa, G. (2018). Priest Sued for Defilement Attempt. *Daily Nation*, September 19, no. 19437.

Cabral, K. (2017) Tough Childhood? The Effects of Trauma on Your Brain. *Anxiety and Stress Counselling, Harley Therapy* 01(26). Retrieved from https://www.harleytherapy.co.uk/counselling/childhood-effects-of-trauma.htm.

Carballo, J. R. (2013). Over 3,000 Religious Leave Consecrated Life Each Year. *Catholic World News*. Retrieved from https://www.catholicculture.org/news/headlines/index.cfm?storyid=19526.

Carballo, J. R. & Braz de Aviz, J. (2017). *New Wine in New Wineskins: The Consecrated Life and Its Ongoing Challenges since Vatican II*. Libreria Editrice Vaticana. Translated in 2018 by Bernadette M. Reis & Reginald Cruz. Nairobi, Kenya: Paulines Publications Africa.

Carlson, J. & Slavic, M. A. (Eds.) (2013). *Techniques in Adlerian Psychology*. New York: Routledge.

Carney, A, G. & Merrell, K. W. (2001). Bullying in Schools: Perspectives on Understanding and Preventing an International Problem. *School Psychology International, 22,* 364—382.

Carothers, S. S., Borkowski, J. G., Lefever, J. B., & Whitman, T. L. (2005). Religiosity and the Socioemotional Adjustment of Adolescent Mothers and their Children. Journal of *Family Psychology*, 19(2), 263-275.

Cartwright, K. B. (2001). Cognitive Developmental Theory and Spiritual Development. *Journal of Adult Development,* 8(4), 213-220.

Catechism of the Catholic Church. Retrieved from http://www.vatican.va/archive/ccc_css/archive/catechism/p1s1c3a1.htm

Catholic World News, (2017). Pope Francis Discusses 'Haemorrhage' of Religious Vocations. Retrieved from https://www.catholicculture.org/news/headlines/index.cfm?storyid=30606.

Charles, S. T., Reynolds, C. A., & Gatz, M. (2001). Age-Related Differences and Change in Positive and Negative Affect over 23 Years. *Journal of Personality and Social Psychology, 80,* 136–151.

Coles, R. (1990). *The Spiritual Life of Children.* Boston: Houghton.

Collins, R. M. (2017). *Called by God: Discernment and Preparation for Religious Life.* Steubenville, Ohio: Emmaus Road Publishing.

Corey, G. (2009). *Theory and Practice of Counselling and Psychotherapy,* (8th Ed). Belmont, CA: Thompson Brooks/Cole.

Corey, G. (2013). *Theory and Practice of Counselling and Psychotherapy,* (9th Ed). Belmont, CA: Cengage Learning.

Corey, G. (2015). *Theory and Practice of Counselling and Psychotherapy,* (10th Ed). Belmont, CA: Cengage Learning.

Corsaro, W. A. (2005). *The Sociology of Childhood,* 2nd Edition. Thousand Oaks, CA: Sage Publications.

Coyle, A. (2011). Critical Responses to Faith Development Theory: A Useful Agenda for Change? *Archive for the Psychology of Religion,* 33(3), 281-298.

Creswell, J. W. (2013). *Research Design.* Los Angeles: Sage Publication, Inc.

Creswell, J. W. (2014). *Understanding Mixed Method Research.* Retrieved from https://www.researchgate.net/file.PostFileLoader.html?id=55eb95f16307d984de8b4584&assetKey=AS%3A273846907670528%401442301598571

Davis, R. (2016). Journeying Through Physical Health. In Barbara Douglas, Ray Woolfe, Sheelagh Strawbridge, Elaine Kasket & Victoria Galbraith, (Eds.) *The Handbook of Counselling Psychology*, 4th Edition (pp. 479-495). Thousand Oaks, CA: Sage Publications.

Dawson, C. (2002). *Practical Research Methods: A User-Friendly Guide to Mastering Research Techniques and Projects.* United Kingdom: Howtobooks.

Day, J. M. (2001). From Structuralism to Eternity? Re-Imagining the Psychology of Religious Development after the Cognitive-Developmental Paradigm. *International Journal for the Psychology of Religion,* 11(3), 173-183.

De Lame, D. (2010). Grey Nairobi: Sketches of Urban Socialites. In Helen Charton-Bigot & Deyssi Rodriguez-Torres (Eds.) *Nairobi Today: A Paradox of a Fragmented City*, (pp. 167-214). Dar es Salam, Tanzania: Mkuki na Nyota Publishers.

Denzin, N.K. and Lincoln, Y.S. (eds) (2000). *Handbook of Qualitative Research*, 2nd Edition. Thousand Oaks, CA: Sage Publications.

Dodge, K. A. (1991). Emotion and Social Information Processing. In J. Garber & K. A. Dodge (Eds.) *The Development of Emotion*

Regulation and Dysregulation (pp. 159-181). New York: Cambridge University Press.

Draucker, C. B. & Martsolf, D. (2006). *Counselling Survivors of Childhood Sexual Abuse*, 3rd Ed. London: Sage Publication.

Dunkel, C., & Sefcek, J. (2009). Eriksonian Lifespan Theory and Life History Theory: An Integration using the Example of Identity Formation. *Review of General Psychology, 13*(1), 13-23.

Elkind, D. (1961). The Child's Conception of His Religious Denomination I: The Jewish Child. *Journal of Genetic Psychology*, 99, 209-225.

_____. (1962). The Child's Conceptions of his Religious Denomination II: The Catholic Child. *Journal of Genetic Psychology*, 101, 185-193.

_____. (1963). The Child's Conceptions of his Religious Denomination III: The Protestant Child. *Journal of Genetic Psychology*, 103, 291-304.

_____. (1964a). The Child's Conception of His Religious Identity. *Lumen Vitae*, 19, 635-646.

_____. (1964b). Piaget's Semi-Clinical Interview and the Study of Spontaneous Religion. *Journal for the Scientific Study of Religion*, 4, 40-46.

_____. (1970). The Origins of Religion in the Child. *Review of Religious Research*, 12, 35-42.

_____. (1971). The Development of Religious Understanding in Children and Adolescents. In M. P. Strommen (Ed.), *Research in Religious Development* (pp. 655-685). New York: Hawthorn Books.

Ellis, A. (2001). *Overcoming Destructive Beliefs, Feelings, and Behaviours: New Directions for Rational Emotive Behaviour Therapy*. New York: Prometheus Books.

Ellis, A., Abrams, M., & Abrams, L. D. (2009). *Personality Theories: Critical Perspectives*. Thousand Oaks, CA: Sage Publication.

Erikson, E. H. (1950). *Childhood and society*. New York: Norton.

Erikson, E. H. (1959) *Identity and the Life Cycle*. New York: International University Press.

Erikson, E. H. (1968). *Identity: Youth and Crisis*. New York: Norton.

Erskine, R. G. & Moursund, J. P. (2011). *Integrative Psychotherapy in Action*. London: Karnao Books Ltd.

Eysenck, M. C. (2004). *Psychology: An International Perspective*. New York: Psychology Press.

Ezeani, C. C. (2017). When You Leave Religious Life, What Then? Accompanying Persons in the Process of Discontinuation from Religious Formation. *UISG Bulletin*, no. 162. Retrieved from www.internationalunionsuperiorsgeneral.org/leave-religious-life/. (This article was also published in *Religious Life Review*, Vol. 55, no. 300, Sept. 2016).

Feltham, C. (1995). *What is Counselling? The Promise and the Problem of the Talking Therapies*. London: Sage Publications.

Feltham, C., & Dryden, W. (2004). *Dictionary of Counselling*, 2nd Edition. New Jersey: Wiley Publishing Company.

Fisher, S., & Greenberg, R. P. (1996). *Freud Scientifically Reappraised: Testing the Theories and Therapy*. John Wiley & Sons.

Ford-Grabowsky, M. (1987). Flaws in Faith Development Theory. *Religious Education*, 82(1), 80-93.

Ford-Martin, P. (2001). Sigmund Freud. In Bonnie B. Strickland (Ed.), *The Gale Encyclopaedia of Psychology* (p. 261), 2nd Edition. Detroit, MI: Gale Group.

Fowler, J. W. (1981). *Stages of Faith: The Psychology of Human Development and the Quest for Meaning.* San Francisco: Harper & Row.

Fowler, J. W. (1986). Faith and the Structuring of Meaning. In Dykstra, C. & Parks, S. (Eds). *Faith Development and Fowler* (pp. 15–42). Birmingham, Alabama: Religious Education Press.

Fowler, J. W. (1987). *Faith Development and Pastoral Care.* Philadelphia: Fortress.

Fowler, J. W. (1991). *Weaving the New Creation: Faith Development and Public Church.* San Francisco, CA: Harper & Row.

Fowler, J. W. (2000). *Becoming Adult, Becoming Christian: Adult Development and Christian Faith.* San Francisco, CA: Jossey-Bass Publishers.

Fowler, J. W. (2001). Faith Development Theory and the Postmodern Challenges. *International Journal for the Psychology of Religion,* 11(3), 159-172.

Fowler, J.W. (2004). Faith Development at 30: Naming the Challenges of Faith in a New Millennium. *Religious Education,* 99(4), 405-421.

Fowler, J. W., & Dell, M. (2005). Stages of Faith from Infancy through Adolescence: Reflections on Three Decades of Faith Development Theory. In E. C. Roehlkepartain, P. E. King, L.

Wagener, & P. L. Benson (Eds.), *The Handbook of Spiritual Development in Childhood and Adolescence* (pp. 35-46). Thousand Oaks, CA: Sage Publication.

Fowler, J. W. & Keen, S. (1978). *Life Maps: Conversations on the Journey of Faith.* (Ed.) Jerome Berryman. Waco, TX: Word Books.

Freud, A. (1936). *The Ego and the Mechanisms of Defense.* London: Hogarth Press and Institute of Psycho-Analysis.

Freud, S. (1900). The Interpretation of Dreams, Retrieved from http://psychclassics.yorku.ca/Freud/Dreams/dreams.pdf

Freud, S. (1915). *The Unconscious.* Standard Edition, 14: 159-204.

Freud, S. (1920). *Beyond the Pleasure Principle.* Standard Edition, 18: 1-64.

Freud, S. (1923). *The Ego and the Id.* Standard Edition, 19: 1-66.

Freud, S. (1933). *New Introductory Lectures on Psychoanalysis.* London: Hogarth Press and Institute of Psycho-Analysis. Pp. xi + 240.

Freud, S. (1961). The resistances to psycho-analysis. *In The Standard Edition of the Complete Psychological Works of Sigmund Freud, Volume XIX* (1923-1925): The Ego and the Id and other works (pp. 211-224).

Frydenberg, E. (1997). *Adolescent Coping: Theoretical & Research Perspectives.* New York: Routledge.

Gilmore, K. & Meersand, P. (2014). *Normal Child and Adolescent Development: A Psychodynamic Primer.* Washington, DC: American Psychiatric Publishing.

Gitau, M. (2016). Formation of Consecrated Persons in East Africa: Contexts, Struggles and Possibilities. In Consecrated Life in Africa: Yesterday, Today and Tomorrow, (pp. 125-148). Nairobi, Kenya: Paulines Publications Africa.

Glaser, D. (2002). Emotional Abuse and Neglect (Psychological Maltreatment): A Conceptual Framework. *Child Abuse & Neglect, 26*, 697-714.

Glesne, C. (2006). *Becoming Qualitative Researchers: An Introduction*, 3rd Edition. New York: Allyn & Bacon.

Glew, G., Rivara, E, & Feudtner, C. (2000). Bullying: Children Hurting Children. *Pediatrics in Review, 21,* 183-190.

Goldman, R. (1964). *Religious Thinking from Childhood to Adolescence*. London: Routledge and Kegan Paul.

Goldman, R. (1965). *Readiness for Religion: A Basis for Developmental Religious Education*. New York: The Seabury Press.

Goodman, M. L., Grouls, A., Chen, C. X., Keiser, P. H., & Gitari, S. (2016). Adverse Childhood Experiences Predict Alcohol Consumption Patterns among Kenyan Mothers. *Substance Use & Misuse Journal,* 52(5), 632-638.

Goodman, M. L., Gutarra, C., Billingsley, K. M., Keiser, P. H., & Gitari, S. (2017). Childhood Exposure to Emotional Abuse and Later Life Stress among Kenyan Women: A Mediation Analysis of Cross-Sectional Data. *An International Journal*, 30(4), 469-483.

Gratton, C., & Ian, J. (2010). *Research Methods for Sports Studies*. 2nd Edition. New York: Routledge.

Gravetter, F. J., & Forzano, L. B. (2012). *Research Methods for the Behavioural Sciences*, 4th Edition. Belmont, CA: Wadsworth Cengage Learning.

Gravetter F. J., & Wallnau, L. B. (2008). *Essentials of Statistics for the Behavioural Sciences*, 6th Edition. Belmont, CA: Thomson Wadsworth.

Guimaraes, F. (2001). *Research: Anyone Can Do It*. Mainz, Germany: PediaPress.

Gupta, R., Kilby, M., & Cooper, G. (2008). Fetal Surgery and Anaesthetic Implications. *Continuing Education in Anaesthesia, Critical Care & Pain*, 8(2), 71-75.

Gyimah, S. O., Kodzi, I., Emina, J., Cofie, N., & Ezeh, A. (2013). Religion, Religiosity and Premarital Sexual Attitudes of Young People in the Informal Settlements of Nairobi, Kenya. *Journal of Biosocial Science*, 45, 13-29.

Hayes, S. C., Follette, V. M., & Linehan, M. M. (2011). *Mindfulness and Acceptance: Expanding the Cognitive Behavioural Tradition*. New York: The Guilford Press.

Heywood, D. (2008). Faith Development Theory: A Case for Paradigm Change. *Journal of Beliefs & Values*, 29(3), 263-272.

Hoehn, R. A. (1983). Book Review: Stages of Faith. In *Review of Religious Research*,25(1), 78-87.

Hood, R. W. (2003). Spirituality and Religion. In A. L. Greil & D. G. Bromley (Eds.), *Religion: Critical Approaches to Drawing Boundaries between Sacred and Secular* (pp. 241-264). Amsterdam: Elsevier.

Hook, D. (2002). Erikson's Psychosocial Stages of Development. In Jacki Watts, Kate Cockcroft, and Duncan N. (Eds.), *Developmental Psychology*, 2nd Edition, (283-312). South Africa: UCT Press.

Horowitz, J. & Dias, E. (2019). "Pope Acknowledges Nuns Were Sexually Abused by Priests and Bishops." *The New York Times*, February 5th. Retrieved from https://www.nytimes.com/2019/02/05/world/europe/pope-nuns-sexual-abuse.html.

Hyatt, M. (2011). "It Is as You Chose It to Be." Retrieved from https://michaelhyatt.com/it-is-as-you-chose-it-to-be/.

Hyde, K. E. (1968). A Critique of Goldman's Research. *Religious Education*, 63, 429-434.

_____. (1990). *Religion in Childhood and Adolescence: A Comprehensive Review of Research*. Birmingham, AL: Religious Education Press.

Jardine, M. M. & Viljoen, H. G. (1992). Fowler's Theory of Faith Development: An Evaluative Discussion. *Religious Education*, 87(1), 74-85.

Johnson, A. (2014). Kenya: Geography, Culture, and Economics. *Borgen Magazine*, January Edition. Retrieved from www.borgenmagazine.com/kenya-geography-culture-economics.

Kabiru, C. W., Elung'ata, P., Mojola, S. A., & Beguy, D. (2014). Adverse Life Events and Delinquent Behaviour among Kenyan Adolescents: A Cross-Sectional Study on the Protective Role of Parental Monitoring, Religiosity, and Self-Esteem. *Child and Adolescent Psychiatry and Mental Health*, 8(24). Retrieved from https://capmh.biomedcentral.com/articles/10.1186/1753-2000-8-24.

Kagwanja, P. & Southall, R. (2010). "Introduction: Kenya-A democracy in Retreat?" In P. Kagwanja, & R. Southall (Ed.), *Kenya's Uncertain Democracy: The Electoral Crisis of 2008*, (pp. 1-19). New York: Routledge.

Kakah, M. (2014). "Priest Killed Bishop, gets Death Sentence." *Daily Nation*. Retrieved from https://www.nation.co.ke/news/Bishop-Luigi-Locati-Murder-Sentence/1056-2513840-k9251g/index.html.

Keller, B. & Streib, H. (2013). Faith Development, Religious Styles and Biographical Narratives: Methodological Perspectives. *Journal of Empirical Theology*, 26, 1-21.

Kerlinger, F. N. (1970) *Foundations of Behavioural Research*. New York: Holt, Rinehart & Winston.

Kenya Catholic Secretariat. (2006). *Kenya Catholic Directory*. Nairobi, Kenya: KCD Datacentre.

Kenya Demographics Profile (2018). Retrieved from https://www.indexmundi.com/kenya/demographics_profile.html

Kenya Psychological Association (2002). The Kenya Psychological Association Code of Ethics. Retrieved from http://www.kpsya.or.ke/resources/finish/3-code-of-ethics/11-kpsya-ethics-code.html.

Khera, S. (2014). *You Can Win: A Step-By-Step Tool for Top Achievers*. India: Bloomsbury Publishing Limited.

Kiprotich, A. (2009). "It's not Just the Priests, Nuns too Break the Vows." *The Standard.* Retrieved from https://www.standardmedia.co.ke/business/article/1144018049/it-s-not-just-the-priests-nuns-too-break-the-vow.

Korniejczuk, V. A. (1993). "Psychological Theories of Religious Development: A Seventh-Day Adventist Perspective, Institute for Christian Teaching, Silver Spring, MD. Retrieved from http://circle.adventist.org/files/CD2008/CD1/ict/vol_10/10cc_257-276.pdf.

Kyule, T., (2013). "Introduction to University Studies." In J. Kyule, J. Lukwala, & C. Majawa (Eds), *A Guide to Research Work and University Studies for the Faculty of Theology*, (pp. 33-59). Nairobi, Kenya: CUEA Press.

Lewis-Morrarty, E., Degnan, K. A., Chronis-Tuscano, A., Pine, D. S., Henderson, H. A., & Fox, N. A. (2015). Infant Attachment Security and Early Childhood Behavioral Inhibition Interact to Predict Adolescent Social Anxiety Symptoms. *Child Development*, 86(2), 598–613.

Lindridge, A. (2008). Spirituality Matters. *Mental Health Today*, 30-33. Retrieved from http://www.ncbi.nlm.nih.gov/pubmed/18165982.

Logan, R. D. (1986). A Reconceptualization of Erikson's Theory: The Repetition of Existential and Instrumental Themes. *Human Development, 29*, 125–136.

Loken, M. H. & Reigstad, H. L. (2012). Associations between Childhood Trauma, Childhood Sexual Abuse, and Adult Psychological Symptomatology. Department of Clinical Psychology, University of Bergen. Retrieved from http://bora.uib.no/bitstream/handle/1956/6432/101805842.pdf?sequence=1.

Macfie, B. P., & Nufrio, P. M. (2006). *Applied Statistics for Public Policy*. New York: M. E. Sharp, Inc.

Maganya, I. (2016). "Doing Formation in East Africa." In *Consecrated Life in Africa: Yesterday, Today and Tomorrow*, (pp. 141-146). A Symposium organized by Tangaza University College, Nairobi, from 23-26th September, 2015. Nairobi, Kenya: Paulines Publications Africa.

Marcato, J. S. (2000). "Experiences of God: The Faith, Spirituality, and Concepts of Religion among Generation X Roman Catholics." Ph.D. Diss., Boston College.

Marshall, C., & Rossman, G., (2011). *Designing Qualitative Research*. 5th Edition. Thousand Oaks, CA: Sage Publications.

Mathers, N., Fox, N. & Hunn, A. (2009). Surveys and Questionnaires. Retrieved from https://www.rds-yh.nihr.ac.uk/wp-content/uploads/2013/05/12_Surveys_and_Questionnaires_Revision_2009.pdf.

McDargh, J. (2001). Faith Development Theory and the Postmodern Problem of Foundations. *International Journal for the Psychology of Religion*, 11(3), 185-199.

McGrath, A. (2004). *The Science of God*. London: T & T Clark/Wm. B. Eerdmans.

McLeod, S. A. (2009). Defense mechanisms. Retrieved from www.simplypsychology.org/defense-mechanisms.html

McLeod, S. A. (2013). "Erik Erikson." Retrieved from www.simplypsychology.org/Erik-Erikson.html.

McLeod, S. A. (2013). Sigmund Freud. Retrieved from www.simplypsychology.org/Sigmund-Freud.html

McMinn, M. R. (2008). *Cognitive Therapy Techniques in Christian Counselling*. Eugene, OR: Word Publishers.

McNamara, B., & McNamara, E. (1997). *Keys to Dealing with Bullies*. Hauppauge, NY: Barron's.

Messman-Moore, T. L., & Coates, A. A. (2007). The Impact of Childhood Psychological Abuse on Adult Interpersonal Conflict. *Journal of Emotional Abuse, 7*(2), 75-92.

Mijares, S. G., & Khalsa, G. S. (2005). Introduction. In Sharon G. Mijares & Gurucharan S. Khalsa (Eds.) *The Psychospiritual Clinician's Handbook: Alternative Methods for Understanding and Treating Mental Disorders*, (1-12). New York: Haworth Press, Inc.

Moore, K., Gomez-Garibello, C., Bosacki, S., & Talwar, V. (2016). Children's Spiritual Lives: The Development of a Children's Spirituality Measure. *Religions,* 7(95), 1-11.

Muhangi, A., Munene, A., & Ssibetya, B. N. (2017). "Innocent Prisoners: Early Childhood Care and Development of Young Children Living with their Mothers in Prison in Uganda and Kenya." *Childhood in Africa: An Interdisciplinary Journal*, Ohio University, 4(1), 11-22.

Musisi, H. D. & Ochen, E. A. (2017). "The Care and Support of Vulnerable Children by Foster Care Families in Uganda: Lessons in Social Justice and Social Protection." *Childhood in Africa: An Interdisciplinary Journal*, Ohio University, 4(1), 33-43.

Mvungu, E. N. (2014). "Societal Factors and Behaviour Maladjustment of the Boy-Child: A Case of Boys in Selected Rehabilitation Institutions in Nairobi and Kiambu Counties, Kenya." A Ph.D. Diss., Kenyatta University, Nairobi, Kenya.

Myers, J. E., & Sweeney, T. J. (2008). Wellness Counselling: The Evidence Base for Practice. *Journal of Counselling and Development*, 86, 482-493.

NanseI, T. R., Overpeck. M., Pilla, R. S., Ruan. W. J., Simons-Morton, B., & Scheidt, R. (2001). Bullying Behaviors among US Youth: Prevalence and Association with Psychosocial Adjustment. *JAMA*, 285, 2094-2110.

National School Safety Center. (1995). *School Bullying and Victimization.* Malibu, CA: Author.

Nelson, J. M. (2009*). Psychology, Religion, and Spirituality.* New York: Springer.

Neuman, M. E. (2011). Addressing Children's Beliefs through Fowler's Stages of Faith. *Journal of Pediatric Nursing*, 26(1), 44-50.

Ngollo J. & Kilanga, T. (2018). "Mourners Pay Last Respects to Nun." *The Citizen.* Retrieved from http://www.thecitizen.co.tz/News/Mourners-pay-last-respects-to-nun-/1840340-4735040-34iyygz/index.html.

Nicolson, P. (2010). *Domestic Violence & Psychology: A Critical Perspective.* New York: Routledge.

Ogbuji, A. H. (2015). *Dealing Effectively with Domestic Abuse: The Ministry of Reconciliation and Healing.* Nairobi, Kenya: CUEA Press.

Okeyo, V. (2017). "Abuse, Neglect Batter Lives of Kenyan Children." *Daily Nation*, March 27, 2017. Retrieved from https://www.nation.co.ke/health/Abuse--neglect-pound-lives-of-Kenyan-children-/3476990-3866918-15n4i0tz/index.html.

Okpalaenwe, N. E. (2014). *Psychological Counselling for Africa: Handbook on Psychotherapy and Cultural Counselling in African Contexts.* Nairobi, Kenya: CUEA Press.

Oladeji, B. D., Makanjuola, V. A., & Gureje, O. (2010). "Family-Related Adverse Childhood Experiences as Risk Factors for Psychiatric Disorders in Nigeria." *The British Journal of Psychiatry*, 196(3), 186–191.

Olweus, D. (1993). *Bullying at School: What We Know and What We Can Do.* Cambridge, MA: Blackwell.

Ombati, C. (2011). "Catholic Nun Burns Herself to Death." *The Standard*. Retrieved from https://www.standardmedia.co.ke/article/2000027936/catholic-nun-burns-herself-to-death

O'Reilly, L. (2013). *The Impact of Vatican II on Women Religious: Case Study of the Union of Irish Presentation Sisters.* United Kingdom: Cambridge Scholars Publishing.

O'Reilly, M. L. (2004). Spirituality and Mental Health Clients. *Journal of Psychosocial Nursing and Mental Health Services*, 42(7), 44-53.

Pagano, R. R. (2013). *Understanding Statistics in the Behavioural Sciences*, 10th Edition. Belmont, CA: Wadsworth Cengage Learning.

Pargament, K. I. (1997). *The Psychology of Religion and Coping: Theory, Research and Practice.* New York: Guilford Press.

Parker, S. (2006). Measuring Faith Development. *Journal of Psychology and Theology*, 34(4), 337-348.

Parker, S. (2013). Research in Fowler's Faith Development Theory: A Review Article. *Review of Religious Research,* 51(3), 233-252.

Parks, S. D. (1992). Faith Development in a Changing World. In Jeff Astley and Leslie Francis (Eds.) *Christian Perspectives on Faith Development: A Reader* (pp. 92-106). Grand Rapids, MI: William B. Eerdmans Publishing Company.

Pastorino, E., & Doyle-Portillo, S. (2014). *What Is Psychology? Foundations, Applications and Integration.* Boston, MA: Cengage Learning.

Paul, M. K. "Achieving Personal Greatness." Retrieved from http://frjoedabreo.com/pdfs/ACHIEVING%20PERSONAL%20GREATNESS%20with%20pictures_book2.pdf.

Pearce, M. J., Koenig, H. G., Robins, C. J., Nelson, B., Shaw, S. F., Cohen, H. J., & King, M. B. (2015). Religiously Integrated Cognitive Behavioral Therapy: A New Method of Treatment for Major Depression in Patients with Chronic Medical Illness. *Psychotherapy (Chic)* 52(1): 56–66.

Pettit, G. S., Dodge, K. A., & Brown, M. M. (1988). Early Family Experience, Social Problem Solving Patterns, and Children's Social Competence. *Child Development, 59* (1), 107-120.

Piaget, J. (1932). *The Moral Judgment of the Child.* London: Routledge.

_____. (1952). *The Origins of Intelligence in Children.* New York: International Universities Press.

_____. (1967). *Six Psychological Studies.* New York: Vintage Books.

Piaget, J., & Inhelder, B. (1969). *The Psychology of the Child.* New York: Basic Books.

Piedmont, R. (2007). Cross-Cultural Generalizability of the Spiritual Transcendence Scale to the Philippines: Spirituality as a Human Universal. *Mental Health, Religion and Culture*, 10, 89-107.

Pope Francis. (2014). "Rejoice! A Letter to Consecrated Men and Women," Retrieved fromhttp://www.vatican.va/roman_curia/congregations/ccscrlife/documents/rc_con_ccscrlife_doc_20140202_rallegratevi-lettera-consacrati_en.html.

Pope Francis. (2014). Pope Francis addresses seminarians from the Pontifical Roman Universities. Retrieved from https://www.catholicnewsagency.com/news/29619/gossip-is-the-plague-of-community-life-pope-tells-seminarians.

Pope Francis. (2014). Apostolic Letter to all Consecrated People, On the Occasion of the Year of Consecrated Life. Retrieved from, https://www.vatican.va/content/francesco/en/apost_letters/documents/papa-francesco_lettera-ap_20141121_lettera-consacrati.html.

Pope Francis. (2017). How To Have Hope: Pope Francis Gives Point-by-Point Guide. *National Catholic Reporter*. Retrieved from https://www.ncronline.org/news/vatican/how-have-hope-pope-francis-gives-point-point-guide.

Pope Francis. (2024). Dilexit nos: On the Human and Divine Love of the Heart of Jesus Christ. Accessed from https://www.vatican.va/content/francesco/en/encyclicals/documents/20241024-enciclica-dilexit-nos.html.

Ratcliff, D. (1985). The Development of Children's Religious Concepts: Research Review. *Journal of Psychology and Christianity*, 4, 35-43.

Regnerus, M. D., & Elder, G. H. (2003). Staying on Track in School: Religious Influences in High and Low-risk Settings. *Journal for the Scientific Study of Religion*, 42, 633–649.

Rizzuto, A. M. (1979). *The Birth of the Living God*. Chicago: The University of Chicago Press.

Rogers, C. (1959). A Theory of Therapy, Personality and Interpersonal Relationships as Developed in the Client-Centered Framework. In S. Koch, (Ed.), *Psychology: A Study of a Science. Vol. 3: Formulations of the person and the social context*. New York: McGraw Hill.

Ruiter, S., & Tubergen, F. V. (2009). Religious Attendance in Cross-National Perspective: A Multilevel Analysis of 60 Countries. *American Journal of Sociology*, 115(3), 863-895.

Sacks, V., Murphy, D., & Moore, K. (2014). Adverse Childhood Experiences: National and State Level Prevalence. *Child Trends*, 28.

Sangawi, S. H., Adams, J., & Reissland, N. (2015). The Effects of Parenting Styles on Behavioural Problems in Primary School Children: A Cross-Cultural Review. *Asian Social Science*, 11(22), 20-34.

Scheck, S. (2005). *Stages of Psychosocial Development According to Erik H. Erikson*. Germany: Grin Verlag.

Schermer, V. L. (2003). *Spirit and Psyche: A New Paradigm for Psychology, Psychoanalysis, and Psychotherapy*. New York: Jessica Kingsley Publishers.

Schultz, D. P., & Schultz, S. E. (2009). *Theories of Personality*, 9th ed. New York. Wadsworth.

Shafranske, E. P., & Sperry, L. (2005). Addressing the Spiritual Dimension in Psychotherapy: Introduction and Overview. In L. Sperry & E. P. Shafrankske (Eds.), *Spiritually-Oriented Psychotherapy* (pp. 11-29). Washington, DC: American Psychological Association.

Smith, R. B. (2017). Divorced from Religious Life. *The Catholic World Report*, Dispatch no. 24. Retrieved from www.catholicworldreport.com/2017/08/10/divorced-from-religious-life/.

Smokowski, P. R., & Kopasz, K. H. (2005). Bullying in School: An Overview of Types, Effects,

Family Characteristics, and Intervention Strategies. *Children & Schools,* 27(1), 101-110.

Stephens, L. J. (1998). *Schaum's Outlines of Theory and Problems of Beginning Statistics.* New York: McGraw-Hill.

Streib, H. & Hood, R. W. (2011). Spirituality as Privatized Experience-Oriented Religion: Empirical and Conceptual Perspectives. *Implicit Religion,* 14, 433-453.

Streib, H. (2001). Faith Development Theory Revisited: The Religious Styles Perspective. *The International Journal for the Psychology of Religion, 11*(3), 143–158.

Streib, H. (2003a). Faith Development Research at Twenty Years. In R. R. Osmer & F. Schweitzer (Eds), *Developing a Public Faith: New Directions in Practical Theology* (pp. 15–42). St. Louis, MO: Chalice Press.

Streib, H. (2003b). Variety and Complexity of Religious Development: Perspectives for the 21st Century. In P. H. M. P. Roelofsma, M. T. Jozef, & J. W. Van Saane (Eds), *One Hundred Years of Psychology of Religion* (pp. 123–138). Amsterdam: Vrije University Press.

Streib, H. (2003c). Religion as a Question of Style: Revising the Structural Differentiation of Religion from the Perspective of the Analysis of the Contemporary Pluralistic-Religious Situation. *Journal of Practical Theology*, *7*, 1–22.

Streib, H. (2004). Extending our Vision of Developmental Growth and Engaging in Empirical Scrutiny: Proposals for the Future of Faith Development Theory. *Religious Education*, *99*(4), 427–434.

Streib, H. (2005). Faith Development Research Revisited: Accounting for Diversity in Structure, Content, and Narrativity of Faith. *The International Journal for the Psychology of Religion,* 15(2), 99–121.

Strieb, H. (2013). Heinz Streib on Faith Development Theory. Host, Christopher Silver. *The Religious Studies Project*, Audio file. 04 March. 2013. Retrieved from http://www.religiousstudiesproject.com/podcast/podcast-heinz-streib-on-faith-development-theory/.

Tirch, D., Silberstein, L. R. & Kolts, R. L. (2016). *Buddhist Psychology and Cognitive-Behavioural Therapy: A Clinician's Guide.* New York: The Guilford Press.

Tronick, E. (1975) Still Face Experiment. Accessed from https://www.youtube.com/watch?v=YTTSXc6sARg&pp=ygU6

RHIuIEVkd2FyZCBUcm9uaWNrLCBhbiBBbWVyaWN-hbiBEZXZlbG9wbWVudGFsIFB-zeWNob2xvZ2lzdA%3D%3D).

Tutu, D. (2008). "Brief Meaning of African Word 'UBUNTU.'" Ubuntu Women Institute USA. Accessed from https://uwi-usa.blogspot.com/2012/01/ubuntu-brief-meaning-of-african-word.html.

United States of America Congressional Record. (2012). Proceedings and Debates of the 112th Congress; Second Session. Volume 158—Part 9. July 19, pp. 12852-13187. Washington: United States Government Publishing Office.

Vandevender, A. W. (2012). The Impact of Childhood Experiences on Intrapersonal and Interpersonal Functioning: Does the Past Dictate the Future? Theses and Dissertations, Psychology Department, University of South Carolina. Retrieved from http://scholarcommons.sc.edu/cgi/viewcontent.cgi?article=1006&context=aiken_psychologytheses.

Van der Kolk, B. (2014). *The Body Keeps the Score: Brain, Mind, and Body in the Healing of Trauma.* New York, NY: Viking.

Wald, K. D., & Calhoun-Brown, A. (2007). *Religion and Politics in the United States,* 5th Edition. Lanham, MD: Rowman & Littlefield Publishers, Inc.

Walliman, N., & Baiche, B. (2001). *Your Research Project: A Step-by-step Guide for the First Time Researcher.* London: Sage Publications.

Webster, D. H. (1992). James Fowler's Theory of Faith Development. In Jeff Astley and Leslie Francis (Eds.) *Christian Perspectives on Faith Development: A Reader* (pp. 77-84). Grand Rapids, MI: William B. Eerdmans Publishing Company.

Weiss, N. A. (2012). *Introductory Statistics*, 9th Edition. Boston, MA: Pearson Education, Inc.

Whitley, B. E., & Kite, M. E. (2010). The Psychology of Prejudice and Discrimination. Belmont, CA. Wadsworth.

Wilkins, P. (2010). *Person-Centered Therapy: 100 Key Points*. New York: Routledge.

Winek, J. L. (2009). *Systemic Family Therapy: From Theory to Practice*. Thousand Oaks, CA: Sage Publications.

Winnicott, D. W. (1967). The Location of Cultural Experience. *International Journal of Psycho-Analysis*, 48:368-372.

Wolpe, J. (1964). Behaviour Therapy in Complex Neurotic States. *The British Journal of Psychiatry*, 110(464), 28-34.

Young, J. S., & Cashwell, C. S. (2011). Integrating Spirituality and Religion in Counselling: An Introduction. In C. S. Cashwell & J. S. Young (Eds.) *Integrating Spirituality and Religion into Counselling: A Guide to Competent Practice*, 2nd Edition, (pp. 1-44). Alexandria, VA: John Wiley & Sons Inc.

Zinnbauer, B. J., & Pargament, K. I. (2005). Religiousness and Spirituality. In R. F. Paloutzian & C. L. Park (Eds), *Handbook of the Psychology of Religion and Spirituality* (pp. 21-42). New York: Guilford Press.

Made in the USA
Monee, IL
27 November 2024

71406977R00108